follow the Rabbit-Proof Fence

Nugi Garimara is Doris Pilkington's Aboriginal name. She was born on Balfour Downs Station in the East Pilbara. As a toddler she was removed by authorities from her home at the station, along with her mother Molly Craig and baby sister Anna, and committed to Moore River Native Settlement. This was the same institution Molly had escaped from ten years previously, the account of which is told in *Follow the Rabbit-Proof Fence*.

At eighteen, Doris left the mission system as the first of its members to qualify for the Royal Perth Hospital's nursing aide training program. Following marriage and a family, she studied journalism and worked in film/video production. *Caprice: A Stockman's Daughter*, originally published in 1991, is her first book and won the 1990 David Unaipon National Award. *Follow the Rabbit-Proof Fence* was first published in 1996, and was released internationally in 2002 as the film 'Rabbit-Proof Fence,' directed by Phillip Noyce. Doris's own story is told in *Under the Wintamarra Tree* (UQP, 2002). In 2002 she was appointed Co-Patron of State and Federal Sorry Day Committees' Journey of Healing.

Acclaim for *Follow the Rabbit-Proof Fence*:

"An adventure of great cleverness and courage. To take the journey is to understand something of the scars on the Australian soul."

Tony Stephens, *Age*

"A vividly told story about cultural arrogance, cruelty and courage."

Ian McFarlane, *Canberra Sunday Times*

"This book is almost unbearable to read, and yet is still compulsive."

Juliette Hughes, *Eureka Street*

"Uncontrived and unadorned, Pilkington's story is genuinely moving."

Debra Adelaide, *Sydney Morning Herald*

Comments on the film "Rabbit-Proof Fence":

"It's about the importance of love. About having a heart. About the real people behind the policies and statistics. It's about giving them names, telling their stories. That's what Doris Pilkington Garimara had in mind when she wrote down the story of her mother Molly on which the film is based."

Susie Eisenhuth, *Bulletin*

"A lot of people still don't quite understand the emotions, such as the traumas that one experiences when they are taken away from their parents — the separation and the injustice that occurred back in the 1930s. People who watch this movie will walk away changed more than they may realise."

Cathy Freeman, *Courier-Mail*

"I hope the film will encourage us to reclaim that part of our history for ourselves. It's only by coming to terms with the past, that you can go ahead into the future."

Phillip Noyce, Director of "Rabbit-Proof Fence"

"I could not have written the script without Doris. Without her, it would have been a real outsider's view."

Christine Olsen, Author of "Rabbit-Proof Fence" filmscript

"Sorry, Molly. Sorry, Daisy. Sorry that a book and a movie, inspired by injustice and your bravery, have taken so long to be acknowledged."

Skye Yates, *Daily Telegraph*

DORIS PILKINGTON | NUGI GARIMARA

follow the
Rabbit-Proof
Fence

University of Queensland Press

First published 1996 by University of Queensland Press
Box 6042, St Lucia, Queensland 4067 Australia
Reprinted 2000
Film edition 2002
Reprinted film edition 2002 (twice)
This edition 2002, reprinted 2002, 2003 (three times), 2004, 2005, 2006,
2008, 2009, 2010, 2012, 2013

© Doris Pilkington\Nugi Garimara

Typeset by University of Queensland Press
Printed in Australia by McPherson's Printing Group

www.uqp.com.au

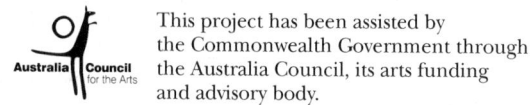

This project has been assisted by
the Commonwealth Government through
the Australia Council, its arts funding
and advisory body.

Sponsored by the Queensland Office
of Arts and Cultural Development.

Cataloguing in Publication Data
National Library of Australia

Pilkington, Doris, 1937– .
    Follow the rabbit-proof fence.

    New ed.

A823.3

ISBN 978 0 7022 3355 5 (pbk)
ISBN 978 0 7022 5204 4 (pdf)
ISBN 978 0 7022 5205 1 (epub)
ISBN 978 0 7022 5206 8 (kindle)

*To all of my mother's and aunty's children
and their descendants for inspiration,
encouragement and determination.*

Contents

Acknowledgments

I gratefully acknowledge my mother and my aunt for sharing this story with me, and the Aboriginal Arts Board for making it possible for me to publish their experience. To those who have advised and supported me in this project, I extend my thanks and appreciation. Special acknowledgments go to Keith Chesson; Jenny Clark, librarian, Aboriginal Affairs Planning Authority; Duncan Graham; Jude Allen, Department of Conservation and Land Management (CALM); and Harry Taylor, Information Research Officer, Adoptions Branch, Department of Community Services.

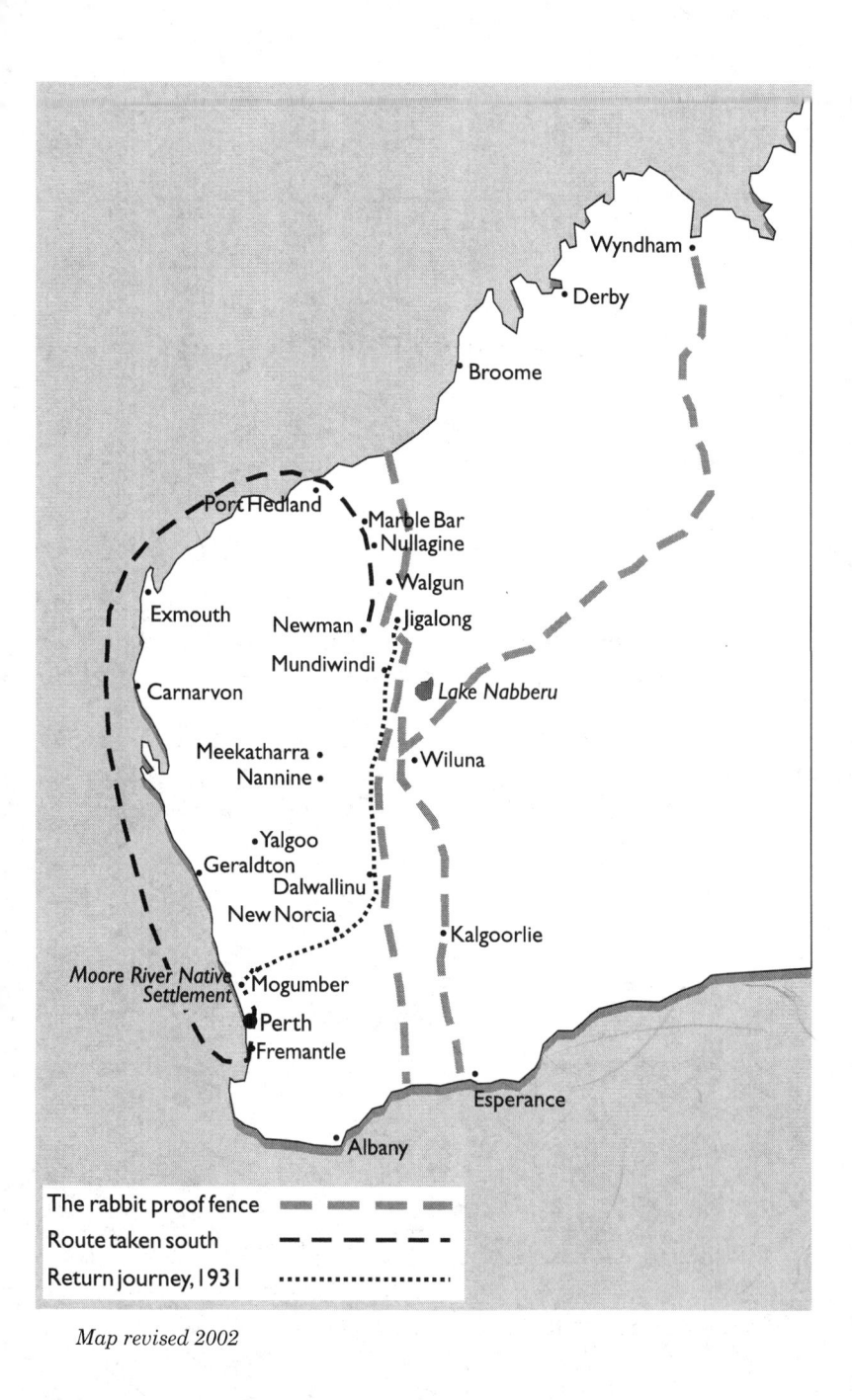

The rabbit proof fence — — — —
Route taken south — — — —
Return journey, 1931 ·····················

Map revised 2002

Introduction

The trek back home to Jigalong in the north-west of Western Australia from the Moore River Native Settlement just north of Perth was not only a historical event, it was also one of the most incredible feats imaginable, undertaken by three Aboriginal girls in the 1930s.

The two surviving members of the trio, my mother and her sister Daisy, are now in their late sixties and seventies and are anxious for their story to be published before they die. They refer to their sister Grace in the interviews simply as "the sister we lose 'em in Geraldton" or "your Aunty". This is the custom in traditional Aboriginal communities where the name of a person is never mentioned after their death. Anyone with the same name is referred to as gurnmanu which means "what's his name", or have Nguberu substituted for their given names. For example, Adam Thomas would be addressed as Nguberu Thomas following the death of another man named Adam.

The task of reconstructing the trek home from the settlement has been both an exhausting and an interesting experience. One needed to have a vivid imagination, the patience of many saints and the determination to succeed despite the odds. Molly, Daisy and Gracie were outside familiar territory so I found it necessary to become a ten-year-old girl again in order to draw on my own childhood memories of the countryside surrounding the settlement. In my mind I walked the same paths and called on my skills as a writer to describe the scenery and how it looked through their eyes. By combining my imagination and the information from records of geographical and botanical explorations undertaken in the area during the early 1900s and later, I was able to build a clearer picture of the vegetation and landscape through which the girls trekked.

There were so many other factors that had to be taken into consideration when telling their story. First, how was I going to reconstruct a landscape which had either changed considerably or disappeared completely. At the time of the event much of the terrain was uncleared virgin bush, a strange, scary wilderness to these three girls who came from the desert regions of Western Australia. In addition to this, there were no major highways linking the towns that were scattered in the country north-east of Perth. Molly, Gracie and Daisy passed through parts of the country that changed every 15 or 20 kilometres, with each change of scenery bringing more tension as food and sustenance became harder to procure. In my mind I actually walked beside them, from the moment they left the girls' dormitory at the settlement all the way home to Jigalong.

Age presented no problem for my mother and aunty. Their minds were sharp and they had no difficulty recounting their experiences along the way, however, I realise that consideration must be given to the time lapse since they were young at the time, and to allow for patches of dimmed memories and sketchy reflections. Another fact I completely overlooked until the interviews began was their illiteracy. This, combined with their lack of numeracy skills, made it impossible to establish measurements accurately. Numbers, dates, in fact mathematics of any kind, have little or no relevance in our traditional Aboriginal society. Nature was their social calendar, everything was measured by events and incidents affected by seasonal changes. For example, summer is pink-eye time when eye problems brought on by the heat, dust and flies flare up. This was the period when station workers took their annual holidays. Pink-eye time was the common term used for weekends and days off from normal duties on the stations in the Pilbara region. The winter or rainy season is yalta or galyu time. Similarly the days of the week were named according to which domestic duties were carried out on: Monday was referred to as washing day, Tuesday was ironing day, Wednesday was mending day, and so on.

Time was also marked by activities of cultural and cere-monial significance. For example, the people in Jigalong and the Gibson Desert regions use a specific event or incident when telling stories. Their stories, whether they be oral history or anecdotes, do not begin in the same way as Western stories: "I remember clearly it was during the Christmas holidays in 1968 when ...", and so on. Rather the speaker will remind the listeners that, "It was galyu time. Galyu everywhere, all the roads were cut off ..." Or, "It was Ngulungga time when we had that big meeting". The listeners know that this was the time when traditional rites and rituals were performed. So in these communities time is based on practical events, incidents and seasons.

When recounting the long walk home, Aunty Daisy men-tioned how they chased emu chicks at the Nannine railway siding south of Meekatharra. She described how the chicks were striped in black and white. By combining research and personal observation I was able to establish that the chicks must have been a certain age and so it would have been either late August or September.

Seasonal time and not numbers is important in recount-ing this journey. Consistent with Aboriginal storytelling style, seasonal time and the features of the natural environ-ment are more important to recounting this journey than are the western notions of time and distance. I have though worked to synthesise these different forms of knowledge to give readers the fullest insight into this historic journey.

This journey took place when there were no highways or sealed roads criss-crossing the continent, only gravel roads or more often, dirt tracks and trails made by carts, sulkies and light, early model cars. The girls avoided these routes, especially where the rabbit-proof fence came near towns such as Sandstone. Walking along the tracks and trails, the girls knew that they would have been too exposed to the white population and their whereabouts would have been immediately reported to the local police.

Molly, Gracie and Daisy came from a remote community in the north-west of Western Australia where the white population tended to stick tightly together, and maintained contact by pedal wireless, telephone and mail. Aware of this the girls aimed to pass by silently and swiftly without being detected and to reach home as fast as they could.

1

The First Military Post

*I*T WAS STILL very cool in the early summer morning; the fresh, clean air he breathed into his lungs felt good. He stood up and stretched his arms above his head then dropped them to his side. He was the first to rise. This was not unusual, Kundilla always woke before anyone else and this morning was no different from any other. He looked slowly around at the sleeping forms covered by warm, animal-skin blankets, lying outside their shelters made from branches and slabs of bark. There was no shortage of trees and shrubs around here, that is why this spot was chosen for the winter camp. Kundilla walked silently to perform his early morning rituals, away from the camp, which was situated in a clearing a hundred metres from the river. On his return he stopped along the banks of the river to pull up the fish traps he had set the previous evening. How peaceful it was, with the sounds of birds twittering high above, amid the leafy branches of the giant river gums, and the occasional splash of the fish in the river. Dawn was his favourite time of day. As the sun rose he could meditate and reflect on the events of the past few days but, more importantly, he could plan future activities without interruption and distraction.

Little did he know that soon devastation and desolation would shatter this tranquil environment; that this pristine forest would echo the anguished cries and the ceaseless weeping of thousands of people — his people — as they were tormented by foreigners and driven off their land.

His long, wavy, grey hair and thick white beard heightened his dignified appearance as he approached the camp carrying two fish traps filled with marrons and gilgies for his family's breakfast. He had power and strength which commanded respect.

Kundilla was satisfied with the results of yesterday's annual scrub firing. This was a special time on the seasonal calendar when his family clans from far around would gather on their territory to set fire to areas of dense undergrowth to flush out any game, such as kangaroos and wallabies, that might be sheltering there. All the men waited in strategic places around the scrub as the animals dashed out in panic. Then they either speared or clubbed them to death. The animal pelts were made into warm cloaks as protection against the bitterly cold winter winds of the south west. The smaller skins were made into skin bags with fur lining the inside to be used for carrying babies and as all-purpose bags.

Kundilla had two wives, the senior wife, Ngingana, had already lit the fire to cook the first meal of the day when he returned. She raked the coals and ashes to one side then dropped the marrons and gilgies on them. When they were cooked she pulled them out with a long green stick and laid them on the gum leaves. As she dusted the ashes from the food she called for everyone to come and eat. This meal was washed down with the cool water drawn from the soak under the thick bullrushes that grew along the river bank. Kundilla's second wife Mardina was breastfeeding their youngest child, Jalda.

Her two teenage sons, Wandani and Binmu, would soon be taken away to join several others who would leave the camp as boys to go through the Law and return as men. She glanced proudly at her sons and felt a pang of sadness. To her they were still boys, surely one more summer wouldn't make any difference. She was only their mother, the tribal elders had already made their decision and there was nothing she could do to change it. Mardina wiped the tears from her eyes then raised her head and continued to feed baby Jalda.

Kundilla's three married sons and their families were camped to the right of them. Others camped nearby, forming a semicircle. There were about sixty people in the group and for the hunters and fishermen this was the place to be right now. Some had travelled for many days from outlying areas to join this group while the food supply was plentiful here. Kundilla had planned to move soon to the mouth of the river so that he and his family could feast on crayfish, crabs, seals and shellfish. They all looked forward to this annual trip to the coast.

After breakfast, Kundilla sat under the shade of a large eucalypt away from the camp and began checking his spears and fishing traps in preparation for the coastal trip. Behind him the sounds of normal, everyday camp life continued: mothers and grandmothers yelling orders to their offspring, children playing games, some fighting and squabbling, others delightedly splashing and diving in the pool. As he reached for the sharpening stone to hone a spear, an ominous sound reverberated through the forest. The peace and tranquility was shattered by a loud boom. Alarmed and frightened, the women snatched up their babies and toddlers and ran to the men.

"What was that?" the people asked their leader. Even the flocks of birds were squawking loudly as they sought refuge in the high canopy of the forest.

"I don't know what that noise was or where it came from," Kundilla replied. "But we will go down and find out," he assured them. He called all the adult men to him and they gathered by a tea-tree clump.

"They're back. They've come to take away our women," he said in a voice filled with passion, anxiety and fear.

"Yes, but what can we do to stop them?" asked Bunyun, his eldest son. "You know what happened the last time they came ashore."

The men nodded as they recalled the incident; it happened to Bunyun's Uncle Tumi and other members of his family who usually camped further along the beach, near the cove. They were shot by the white raiders when they tried to stop them from kidnapping the women. The family were still mourning their dead.

Kundilla and his family had heard how their brothers and uncles were killed by ruthless white pirates, desperados and escaped convicts. Those cruel and murderous men came ashore and stole Aboriginal women and kept them on board their ships as sexual slaves, then murdered them and tossed their bodies into the ocean when their services were no longer required. These renegades made up the crews of the American whaling ships who hunted for whales and seals on the southern coast of Western Australia. Although the brave Nyungar warriors fought gallantly and fearlessly, they were no match for the evil white invaders with their muskets, swords and pistols.

When the invaders encountered the Nyungar people of the Great Southern region, they were pleased to find friendly, hospitable people. At first, the Aboriginal men welcomed the sealers and whalers. They were very interested in the boats in which the crew had rowed ashore. Through sign language they managed to indicate that they were impressed with the timber structure and design of the boats. These unsuspecting men were invited to visit the beach camp of the white crew as a gesture of friendship and goodwill; the women stayed behind, out of sight of the strangers.

The Nyungar made it known to the sealers that they wanted to be taken to an island (now known as Green Island) to collect birds' eggs. The request could not please the devious men more; it was just what they wanted. They readily agreed and took six men to the island and left them there, stranded without food or water. Meanwhile, they returned to the mainland and made a thorough search of the area beyond the sand dunes until they found the Aboriginal people's camp and kidnapped six women who were taken back to the whaling ships where they were brutalised and later murdered.

The whalers and sealers soon realised that the Nyungar people respected and revered them because they believed that these white men were gengas. They set up camps along the coast from Kangaroo Island, along the Great Australian Bight and the shores of Western Australia at what was to be called King George Sound.

Major Edmund Lockyer with a detachment of eighteen soldiers from the 93rd Regiment and fifty convicts were sent to King George Sound (where Albany is now situated) by Governor Darling in New South Wales, to establish a military base. Their aim was to deter renegade convicts, whalers and sealers. They sailed in the brig *Amity* and had been anchored offshore in King George Sound for over a month. On a hot summer day in 1826, Major Lockyer and two of his officers went ashore and climbed the cliffs and explored the harbour. They were delighted with the beauty of the coastal region but were not impressed with the soil.

The loud boom that had startled the Nyungar people was a salute from an eighteen-pounder cannon by the soldiers as they raised the British flag, the Union Jack, for the first time on the shores of Western Australia.

When Kundilla and his three sons reached the coast they weren't sure what to expect. As it was quite warm they decided to rest under the shade; it was here that Kundilla admitted to his sons that he was afraid. Suddenly, they heard voices of men shouting loudly and yelling back and forth. Kundilla and his sons became alarmed. They clambered up the cliffs and hid behind the thick bushes on the rocky ledge. Lying on their stomachs they peered over the edge. They were not prepared for the sight that greeted them. They were confronted not with shouting, cruel men, but different men wearing strange scarlet jackets and others in white, coarse cotton suits. All these men were very pale. "Surely they must be gengas," whispered Kundilla, as he moved closer to the edge of the cliff.

The strangers were speaking in a language the Aboriginal men hadn't heard before. They all had the same pale skin but they had different coloured hair. Some had hair like the colour of dry grass and others like the biguda and some had dark hair like their own. The white men had set up a camp site and settled in.

Kundilla and his sons felt a chill pass over them when they saw the reason for the commotion on the beach below. Two Nyungar men were being escorted by four redcoats to a small boat that would take them out to the brig anchored in the harbour. Later they were surprised and pleased when their countrymen returned, unharmed, to shore.

"These strangers are not here to cause harm," Kundilla said to his sons.

It seemed that the Nyungar men were only kept on board the *Amity* while Major Lockyer and a couple of the officers collected specimens of plants and soil, then they were released. When he realised that the strangers were not kidnappers and murderers, Kundilla decided to return to the camp and give an account of what happened on the coast. He would assure his people that the visitors would not endanger their lives.

The military outpost at Albany lasted five years, during which time the garrison and convicts began to suffer from the effects of isolation, loneliness and boredom. Captain Lockyer felt that they didn't really have the weapons to withstand an attack from the whalers and sealers; he and his men were too vulnerable. Eventually they returned to the growing lively city of Sydney leaving behind the tyranny of remote outpost living. Each day at Albany had been an ordeal for the Europeans, they were happy to see the last of the military post.

2

The Swan River Colony

*T*WO HUNTERS KNELT on the wet ground beside the small, grey doe kangaroo and began pulling their spears from its chest. Hunting in this cold, wet weather was always successful because in the rain, both large and small game are easy prey. Their tracks are clearly seen by the hunters and the animals are generally not so alert, with the weather hampering their vision and hearing. When the hunters' approach is masked by the rain, they can easily move up on their unsuspecting target.

Bidgup lifted the kangaroo onto his shoulders while his younger brother, Meedo, collected the spears and other weapons and they began to walk along the trail for home. They were camping at Boorloo, the tribal land at Yellagonga, a peace loving man, and his people.

Bidgup passed a firm green stick through the shanks of the kangaroo, then, with the help of Meedo, they lifted it onto a limb of a banksia tree. Meedo squatted on the ground beneath the paperbark trees and began looking for sharp cutting stones but before he could select any Yellagonga called everyone to a meeting. All except the babies, the old people and the sick, moved closer to their leader's shelter and stood or sat around the fires, waiting anxiously to hear what he had to tell them.

Yellagonga spoke with a clear voice. "We all know that these strange men, the gengas, have been coming to our land for a long, long time." Everyone nodded.

"My grandfather told me about them when I was a little boy. They usually sailed up the river in small boats, searching for fresh water and food, then left. But these gengas are different. And you know what happened not so long ago when Dayup and the others were invited to follow some of them to the river. The genga leader spoke to our men in his language, so they didn't understand what he said."

Those Nyungar men about whom Yellagonga was speaking had no idea what was happening when they met Captain Fremantle. The Captain told the men, the traditional owners who had gathered on the muddy banks of the river, "My government has advised me to meet with you and discuss this matter with you and seek your approval before giving your country an English name."

Dayup glanced at his kinsmen then stared back at the white man who was speaking. He knew by his manner and the way that the other men kept saluting him that he must be an important man, but what was he saying? Dayup only wished he knew what this stranger was talking about. When Captain Fremantle realised that his words were not being understood he decided to try sign language. This language barrier prevented a formal discussion; how could a stranger indicate in sign language that he was giving a foreign name to their traditional land? It was an impossible task and the Nyungar men became even more confused with the pointing and waving. Nevertheless, Captain Fremantle continued.

"All agreed, er, um gentlemen," he said standing to attention.

The Nyungar men glanced once again at Dayup, who was just as stunned and confused as they were. He put his hands out in front of him and shook his head in despair and frustration. He truly wished that he understood the language. He turned to his kinsmen and told them, "I don't know what he is talking about."

"I take it that we are all agreed and that I have your consent," said Captain Fremantle, nodding to the Nyungar men who stood motionless, staring blankly at him.

"Thank you gentlemen." He stood back, looking resplendent in his naval uniform, and announced in a loud voice, "I name this land Western Australia." Then he raised his eyes to the limestone cliffs and saluted smartly at the flag fluttering in the wind; the red, white and blue of the British Empire.

The gunboat HMS *Challenger* in which Captain Fremantle had arrived remained anchored in the estuary for several weeks. It had been sent ahead of Captain James Stirling and the settlers. The Nyungar people grew accustomed to seeing it there and sometimes watched in silence as members of the crew rowed up and down the river.

"Well, today," said Yellagonga, continuing his message, "Yalbung and Beeboo and their sons were hunting for possums near the river when they heard voices of men and the cries of frightened women. They told me that there were other very strange noises, sounds never heard in this part of the country. All this seemed to be coming from over the sandhills.

"They climbed the sandhills cautiously, crawling through the small shrubs until they reached the top and peered over the dunes. Normally this beach is deserted white, sandy expanse, but instead, a strange sight greeted them. Below, strewn along the shore, was an array of belongings, all sorts of things that these strange people brought with them. What's more, they brought their women with them this time," said Yellagonga.

"What does this mean?" asked Moody, his uncle.

"I don't know," he replied. "Perhaps they were shipwrecked."

What it did mean was that the first European settlers had arrived. Their landing in June 1829, during the wet, winter weather was a disappointing introduction to their new home. There they sat in their fine clothes, huddled together under a canvas shelter and watched glumly as the rain poured down on their trunks containing silk gowns, fine china, mementos and other personal belongings.

"The rain will ruin our furniture and piano," cried one of the women. "Do something, somebody, please. Save them please."

"We're doing our best, ma'am," answered a sailor as he tethered one of the horses to a wooden crate. "We have to bring all the livestock ashore first."

The other women remained silent, there was nothing they could do under the circumstances. Nothing but sit and stare at their precious possessions being soaked by the rain, in a land which was a wilderness to these downhearted ladies and gentlemen.

"Where is the Arcadian land that we heard so much about, the land of rustic paradise?" queried Christopher Marsden, a businessman from London. "This certainly isn't the place."

The others nodded in agreement. "We should never have come, Arthur," said one tearful woman to her husband.

She clung tightly to his arm. Arthur Carberry had joined the new settlers because he wanted to become a member of the landed gentry and fulfil his lifelong ambition. How he had envied his rich country men in the past when he had watched them gallop by in their scarlet jackets, during the fox hunt back home in England. On this desolate beach he looked at the two foxes in the large cages in front of him.

He hoped to find good, fertile land and become very wealthy. His wife tightened her grip on his arm and sniffled tearfully. Carberry patted her hand gently and tried to comfort her, "Captain Stirling made a simple miscalculation, that's all. It couldn't be helped."

A simple miscalculation indeed! What really happened, according to historian Robert Hughes in his book *The Fatal Shore*, was that Captain James Stirling sailing in the *Parmelia*, had been leading a voyage that took over eight months. He was anxious to take possession of a land grant of half a million acres of Nyungar land, which the Colonial Office neither bought nor owned but merely claimed for Britain and the Commonwealth, and a bonus of almost a quarter of a million acres of his own choice on arrival. Once he had settled and established a new colony, he would become its first Lieutenant Governor.

Their sea voyage was almost over. He never anticipated that others might find this location just as appealing as he did, so he was totally unprepared for the sight that greeted him as he approached the mouth of the river. There, anchored in the estuary, was the *Challenger*. The sight of the gunboat under its master, Captain Charles Fremantle, caused him to panic. He was so anxious to make port that he tried to take a short cut and ran his ship, with its cargo and passengers — the first English settlers to this part of the country — onto the rocks. Fortunately, no one was drowned.

Captain Stirling also discovered that his rival, Captain Fremantle, had gone ashore, claimed and took formal possession of not just one hundred thousand acres, but of one million square miles of territorial land, naming it Swan River Colony.

For the European settlers on the beach at what is known today as Cottesloe, the worse was yet to come. The terrain appeared unproductive — thick, tangled creepers grew under foot and when the weather fined up, they were plagued by swarms of mosquitoes and other pests.

3

The Decline of Aboriginal Society

*A*LL THOSE WHO arrived with Captain Stirling, and others who settled before 1830, had the right to choose an area of land wherever they fancied. The best land was taken up by the more wealthy, influential people who had the responsibility of maintaining their customs. They were advised to "keep up their Englishness" at all costs. This meant having picnics, fox hunts and balls. These activities were welcomed by the new landed gentry, who came from working class backgrounds. They delighted in dressing up for these occasions and being regarded as members of a social group which previously they had only observed and perhaps envied from afar.

The more adventurous settlers discovered that further up and beyond the Swan River colony there was an abundance of fertile land in which they could grow anything.

The Nyungar people, and indeed the entire Aboriginal population, grew to realise what the arrival of the European settlers meant for them: it was the destruction of their traditional society and the dispossession of their lands. Bidgup and Meedo complained to Yellagonga after several attempts at unsuccessful hunting trips.

"We can't go down along our hunting trails," Bidgup told him. "They are blocked by fences."

"And when we climbed over the fence, one of those men pointed one of those things — guns — at us and threatened to shoot us if we went in there again," said an irritated Meedo.

"There are huts and farms all over the place. Soon they will drive us all from our lands."

Yellagonga had no answer or words of encouragement for his cousins. He wasn't certain about anything anymore. Where there was once bush, there were now tents, huts or houses. Soon the white people would take his land from him and there would be no recourse for any injustices committed against his people.

Cut off from their natural food source, the Nyungar people expected these white settlers to share some of their food with them.

"We will take a sheep, they have plenty, they won't miss one," said Bidgup. His young brother Meedo agreed.

"If there isn't going to be any sharing of food, we'll help ourselves."

When the brothers were caught spearing a sheep they were the first of many Nyungar men to be brought in to be sentenced under the English law. They received several years imprisonment and were transported to Rottnest Island Penal Colony. Their people stood on the banks of the muddy river as they sailed away to their prison. Their elderly parents and wives and children wept and wailed, while others watched silently as they were shoved roughly, their legs in irons, into a boat and sailed down the river, out to the open sea. They were never seen again. Hundreds of others followed them, bound in chains, across the waters into the unknown. A few escaped, others served their sentences and were returned to their homelands, while others were dropped off in strange towns along the coast. Some men remained incarcerated on the island for the rest of their lives.

The white settlers were a protected species; they were safe with their own laws and had police and soldiers to enforce these rules.

One evening, Moody, Yellagonga's uncle, brought back some distressing news from the people at the Lake Monger and the Nyungar people knew their lives were in serious danger. "A big meeting was held there last week and one man was punished for breaking the white men's law and the troopers came down and took several men away."

It became apparent then, that the Aboriginal social structure was not only crumbling, but it was being totally destroyed.

"It seems," added Moody, "that our laws are not being recognised by these strangers." The Nyungar people were hurt and confused when they were punished for carrying out their own traditional laws, handed down to them by the Dreamtime spirit beings.

"Yet when old man Udja complained to the magistrate that a white man stole his wife, Nella, he was given a bag of flour and told to go home," Moody reminded them. "That old man expected the same form of justice under the white man's law. He never got it."

How many more were pacified with gifts of food? The whites had created two sets of laws; this was very confusing for the Nyungar people to understand and accept. There were unending conflicts between the traditional owners and the white invaders, with reports of merciless killings on both sides. The white settlers used muskets, swords and guns against the Nyungar people, who retaliated with spears. Soon, Aboriginal people all over the state learned to acknowledge the white man's brutal strength and their cruel use of superior weapons and were forced to accept the white system of justice and punishment.

The Europeans ventured further inland and like bushfires out of control, they could not be stopped. Confrontations between Nyungar and the invaders became more frequent and the practice of "might is right" prevailed throughout the colony. Driven off their traditional lands, the Aboriginal people of all areas (except the Central and Western Desert regions) became a dispossessed and devastated race. The people discovered, too late, that the white invaders were human beings and not spirits.

The colonists took advantage of the Aboriginal cultural beliefs to further their own gains. The Nyungar people who once walked tall and proud, now hung their head in sorrow. They had become dispossessed; these teachers and keepers of the traditional Law were prevented from practising it. They had to fight to find ways to return to their secret and sacred sites to perform their dances and other ceremonies that were crucial to their culture and whole way of life.

Their pain and suffering remained hidden and repressed, silent and deep. They remembered the corroborrees and songs that they were forbidden to dance and sing, unless commanded by government officials. No longer would the corroborrees be shared and danced by scores of feet, kicking up the dust in the moonlight around the glowing fires. Warriors with painted bodies and plumes of feathers on their ochre-covered heads would become faded images, buried in the past. The important dates on their seasonal calendars would be forgotten.

The British Colony was said to be an excellent settlement for hiring labourers and most colonists preferred Aboriginal workers to others. "Black servants, I find," wrote George Fletcher Moore in his *Diary of Ten Years*, "are very serviceable in this colony; on them we eventually depend for labour, as we can never afford to pay English servants the high wages they expect, besides feeding them so well. The black fellows receive little more than rice — their simple diet."

As a further insult by the white invaders, an act of goodwill in the form of an annual distribution of blankets to the Aboriginal people was established. This generally occurred on Queen Victoria's birthday. The *Illustrated Melbourne Post* of 20 August 1861, page 9, described this event as, "a sorry return for millions of acres of fertile land of which we have deprived them. But they are grateful for small things and the scanty supply of food and raiment doled out to this miserable remnant of a once numerous people, is received by them with the most lively gratitude."

4

From the Deserts They Came

BY THE 1900s, Western Australia was showing signs of progress and prosperity, especially in the mining and agricultural industries. The farming of sheep, cattle and wheat flourished, so the boundaries of white settlement were extended to meet the demands of the growing overseas markets. This expansion brought many changes — settlements inevitably became towns and soon all available arable land in the south-west and the coastal areas north of Perth was occupied by white settlers. The government introduced a policy allowing large areas of the country to be claimed by European farmers and grants of land were given to the pastoralists to raise sheep and cattle without any provision being made for the traditional owners, the Mardudjara people.

The Mardudjara is comprised of several tribes that once lived on their traditional lands in the desert regions. Each group spoke their own dialect. Today, however, they speak a language which is a combination of the two main dialects: Gududjara and Mandildjara. All traditional people are referred to as Mardu, their language is Mardu wangka. The pastoralists and graziers of the Pilbara region were hospitable towards the Mardudjara people. The station owners and managers trained them to be stockmen and domestic help on their stations and they were soon regarded as excellent horsemen and cattlemen. The women proved to be loyal servants, housemaids and cooks, and during mustering time they displayed other skills such as horseriding and took their turn watching the cattle at night. They did not see this work as exploitation but as a form of kindness shown to them. However, just as in other regions in this vast continent during the pastoral expansion, good working relationships and respect came at a cost. There were incidents of violence and murder; some reported, others were not. But all Aboriginal people were affected by the growth of the rural industry, either by expulsion from traditional lands, sexual exploitation of the women or by the criminal acts of murder and violence committed against them.

The only reported incident of confrontation between the Mardu people of the Western Desert and whites occurred when some white construction workers dug up a sacred site and removed sacred objects. This action led to hostility between the two groups. The Mardu men attacked and speared two of the labourers who had violated their sacred ground. The labourers were part of a large team of workers who were sinking wells along the stock route surveyed by A.W. Canning from 1906 to 1909.

Anger spread through the base camp as the white men buried their dead. The remaining workers retaliated by sneaking up on a group of Mardus and shooting them while they slept in a dry creek bed. The unsuspecting Mardu were travelling through the area and had camped for the night, intending to move the next day. They had no idea that the creek they slept in would be their death bed. The incident occurred between Wells 33 and 62 along the Canning Stock Route sometime between 1906 and 1907.

News of the shootings spread throughout the region. The elders realised that their weapons of wood and stone were no match for the white man's guns. Their spears and boomerangs were effective only in a surprise attack at close range, otherwise their weapons were useless in direct conflict with a group of white avengers. From their secluded look-outs, the Mardu men watched the well sinkers as they worked at their daily tasks. One morning at dawn, they were pleased to see the construction workers rolling up their tents and other belongings and loading them on pack horses and camels. They had completed their section of the 1,610 kilometre chain of wells and were going home.

This meant that the Mardus could move about more freely, however the establishment of the Canning Stock Route affected the subsequent migration south-west, to the Jigalong Depot. Each Mardu family group made their own path through the desert and settled at various locations in the East Pilbara and east to Wiluna and the eastern gold-fields; anywhere the food supply was plentiful and continuous and, more importantly, where they would be sheltered and protected from the avenging white men.

The paths criss-crossed throughout the red desert landscape — the traditional homeland of the Mardudjara people for over 40,000 years. Although they weren't driven off their land, the Mardu chose to move for many reasons. Fear of reprisals against them and their kin was the main reason for their migration south, but the stories of a constant food supply and access to the white man's tobacco were also attractive persuaders.

The migration from the east side of Lake Disappointment occurred in small numbers, in groups of six to twelve people. Dora who was born near Lake Dora in the Great Sandy Desert remembers vividly when she, her mother, sister, and two brothers and seven other members of her family, made a long trail across the dusty desert in the north-east of the current site of the Jigalong Aboriginal community. On the way late one dry summer afternoon, the family were resting in the shade of the ghost gums in the dry creek bed. They hadn't eaten meat for two days; the dogs had chased and caught a skinny doe kangaroo, but that was all gone. So the men were planning to go hunting around the rockhole a few kilometres south of their resting place.

Suddenly one of the lads, a recent initiate, shouted excitedly and pointed to the south-east. "Look over there!"

Everyone stood up and stared with curiosity at the huge, slow moving cloud of red dust.

"What is that thing?" everyone wanted to know, the older ones were shielding their eyes from the glare of the sun.

"It looks like a big mob of some kind," said one of the old men. "Must be that ngubby that brother from Jigalong been talking about. Good mundu."

This was the first time the group had seen the white men droving cattle. They were curious indeed and wanted to get a closer look. The droving team rested and watered their herd at the same rockhole the group intended to visit. Only now it was no longer just a rockhole, it had become a government well that provided water for the drovers and their stock as they travelled south along the dusty trails to the rail heads at Wiluna and Meekatharra or north through the Kimberleys to the port of Wyndham.

"Those white spirit devils got plenty of bullocky, we hungry fullahs, we take one," said Dora's father, Lubin.

"I'll go when it's dark," volunteered his younger brother Golda. He wanted to go alone to prove his skills as a hunter and a provider.

"No. It's too risky, we'd better come with you," said Buggeda, his uncle. Everyone agreed that Golda was the right man for the task. So as soon as it was dark enough Golda, Buggeda and his older brother Juberji sneaked towards the herd of cattle. While his two uncles remained hidden behind some spindly mulga trees, Golda approached a reclining steer, one that seemed to be on its own apart from the main herd, and speared it through the stomach. Before he could remove the spear that was lodged deep within the flesh of the beast, he was shot dead by a drover; the night watchman who was about to have a drink of tea when he saw something moving in the flickering firelight.

"What was that, Ted?" asked the members of the mustering team who came running towards him in their boots and underwear.

"Just a blackfella. I caught him trying to steal one of the young steers," he explained.

"Alright, Jim and Mick you two take his body and put it over near that tree," ordered Tom McIarty, the boss of the team. "There's nothing we can do for the steer except put it out of its misery. Ted, you can do that."

"Alright boss," he said as he placed the rifle barrel in the centre of the steer's head and cocked it.

"No," yelled the boss. "Don't use your rifle, too messy, use my pistol. Here," he said as he passed him the weapon.

"Harley, you'd better gut the steer now but skin it in the morning," the boss told him. Harley James set to work then returned to his swag, blew out his hurricane lamp, and tried to put the sight of the dead Aboriginal man out of his mind. He shut his eyes and waited for sleep to come.

Buggeda and Juberji had watched in horror and disbelief as they saw their nephew fall on the ground, the red blood flowing from his dark chest. The murder had been clearly lit by the glow of the drovers' hurricane lamps. They waited until the early hours of the morning when they felt it was safe to go down and carry his body to the camp.

The next day Golda's family performed the traditional rites and buried the body near some small acacia bushes. When the grave was filled with dry red earth they covered it with large stones and rocks to prevent the dingoes from digging it up. The small clan decided to leave this place and follow other members of their family who had migrated earlier.

When they returned to their camp, they saw that the

droving team were moving slowly westwards, so the desert nomads walked quickly to the well and drank their fill, then replenished their wooden coolamons with water for the trip. A few metres away from the troughs one of the men found the remains of a slaughtered steer, the upper part — the head, neck and rib cage. They were pleased with their find. After a breakfast of grilled beef and water they walked as far as they could before the heat became unbearable. Three of the older women made a wuungku. They shared what was left from the beef and drank a little of the water, and rested until late afternoon then continued the trek. The old men decided that when they reached the Rudall River, or Buungul as it was traditionally called, they would travel east until they reached a station property.

"Then we walk some more," said Dora. "All the kids have yina booger, bark ones." She promised to show those who had never seen yina booga how to make them and what kind of bark was used.

This primitive footwear effectively protected the feet from the burning red sands of the desert. Normally the desert nomads roamed around without any sort of covering on their hardened soles but took care never to walk around during the fierce heat of the day. They usually walked from early morning to noon then would rest under a bough shelter or in the shade of a tree until it grew cool enough to continue their journey.

After several hot summer days of travelling and having barely enough to eat, they arrived at a cool, shady riverbed. While the women set about clearing a camp site, the men sat further along the riverbed and began checking their weapons as they intended to go on another hunting trip at first light in the morning, sometimes known as piccaninny dawn.

Jilba, one of the men, stood up to try out his new spear when he noticed a movement through the mulga trees over the other side of the gibber plains. He didn't raise the alarm until he was sure what it was he was seeing. For a while he couldn't make out what it was. The sun was sinking slowly in the western sky and all he could see was the strange thing heading straight for them.

"Bukala, bukala," he ordered everyone then he cried out again more urgently. The women and children didn't waste time asking why, they got down on their hands and knees and crawled towards the large boulders on the other side of the river and hid. From the safety of the rocks, they sneaked a peek at the life-threatening object. They saw a strange being looming closer and closer; all shivered with fear, the children began to whimper and cling to their mothers.

"It's a big marbu with long kudda," said Dora's mother, Barphada. This was the first time that she had seen one this close. They became very frightened.

As the "marbu" came nearer its kudda bounced up and down. The men aimed their spears ready to throw when it came into close range. Suddenly a man called out in Mardu wangka. He greeted them in a friendly manner and told them not to be frightened.

"This is a horse," he said as he rode towards them.

All eyes were focussed on the stranger. This tall, young man was neither black nor white, they observed. He sounded harmless but they still weren't sure; the women and children remained hidden behind the rocks.

His mother was a Mardu, he explained, but his father was a white man, a wudgebulla named Harry Phillips. He was a muda-muda, a half-caste or part Aborigine, who worked as a stockman on Talawana, a station not far away.

He guided the group to the station where they found some of their relations who had come in from the desert some time ago and decided to stay.

This small band of desert dwellers was immediately introduced and instructed on the preparation of white man's food. Their mayi or damper was larger and whiter than the

24

ones made from seeds. The meat was either boiled, fried, salted or came out of tins. And they were given the most refreshing, and what was to become the most popular drink, billy tea, black or with powdered milk and liberally sweetened with white sugar. This was drunk not only by adults but was cooled and shared with the children. How they all marvelled at all the sights and sounds of a pastoral station. There was nothing in the desert to compare with this kind of food. The desert nomads did not use cooking utensils, they simply drank from the rockholes by scooping the water in their hands or sipping from wooden bowls. The only time their drink was varied was during the warm winter days when the flowers from the desert oak, a type of grevillea, were picked and soaked in coolamons of water to make a sweet drink like cordial or lolly water.

While the new arrivals were enjoying their meal, others who had settled there earlier, rummaged through piles of clothes scattered around the camp for suitable clothing — white man's cast-offs — to cover their naked bodies. They were told that, "the boss and the missus don't like to see neked fullah at this place."

"We gotta cover up everything. All buchiman have to put 'em close on," they informed the newcomers.

They stood around in a circle, staring at the heap of clothing that the boss and the missus and others used to cover their bodies. The desert dwellers were baffled, they could not understand why anyone would be embarrassed or offended by their own nakedness: their normal, natural appearance. These people had roamed about in their own environment naked except for a pubic covering made from human hair. Their bodies were covered only with a salve, a mixture of red ochre and animal fat. This ointment is still believed to protect them from illness and evil spirits but its most common use is to disguise human body odour when hunting. Their bodies are also anointed during ceremonial occasions when their rituals are performed.

After supper, the group inspected the clothing before trying on anything. There was a lot of jesting and clowning going on when they paraded around before the amused onlookers. Gales of laughter rang out as old man Jibaru, the smallest man in the group, put on what must have been the largest trousers in the whole collection. Where and how was he expected to "make kumbu" as the waist came up under his armpits!

Each one had a set or two of clothes and nobody was interested whether they were stylish or fashionable so long as their bodies were covered. It didn't matter to anyone if the clothes were ill-fitting and uncomfortable, the important thing was that they were pleasing the boss and the missus.

Later that evening, someone suggested they might like to have a cool shower and change their clothes, but the group refused very strongly. They had just buried a family member and were still in mourning so they would wear the clothes over their ochre-covered bodies until the symbols painted on them disappeared. Bubinya, the elder of the station community, apologised for the lapse of discretion, and poured himself another mug of tea.

So the shower would have to wait. Meanwhile they made themselves comfortable, sitting around the cast-off bundle of white man's clothing, enjoying the conversation and learning what more their new masters required of them if they decided to settle on the property. The station manager was respected and admired by those already living on the property.

"The wudgebulla he clever man. He got strong marbarn. He catch that jilla and keep 'em that ngubby," said one old man, pointing at the windmill and the tank that was over-flowing with water. Anyone who could capture and incarcerate the jilla, the Dreamtime spirit responsible for the creation of the rivers, lakes and rockholes, must have a very powerful magic indeed. The wanderers from the desert could do nothing but marvel.

Bubinya looked extremely weary but contented in the summer evening. He removed the cotton shirt from his back as the clothes made him feel hot and uncomfortable. "All Mardus cover 'em up everything." Although he had lived on the property for almost a year, he still didn't like wearing clothes but he felt he had to pass on this important advice. Everyone nodded in agreement; they understood that they must now conform to these changes in their lifestyle, obey their new bosses and try not to offend them. They settled down on their government-issue blankets and soon all was quiet and everyone fast asleep.

Early one morning, as the sun was rising in the eastern sky, the small group collected their belongings and decided to continue their journey. It had been two and a half months since they had arrived at Talawana Station and they felt that it was time to move on. They packed enough food to last four days: first they would have to walk east until they reached the rabbit-proof fence then once they found the fence it would be a matter of another two days' walk and they would be reunited with those who had gone before.

Fear and unrest continued to spread across the desert, forcing others to leave their homelands to seek the safety and protection at the government outpost at Jigalong. The numbers of new arrivals to the depot were increasing weekly. News of Golda's murder was still filtering through the desert communities. Who would be next? This was the question they were all asking.

Golda and Dora's father Lubin and his family lived at the depot for over a year and were content to remain there for the rest of their lives. Among the first people to settle at Jigalong were Ruppi and his family. When Lubin discovered this he became interested in their story and the reason why they migrated to the outpost.

"Which way did you come, Ruppi?"

"We came this way," Ruppi said pointing to the south-east. "On the right side of Gumbalbindil." (This is the traditional name of Lake Disappointment in the Gibson Desert.) "Carnegie Station," he added.

Ruppi remembered that it had been an extremely hot day, the salt lakes were simmering with heat and the spindly mulga trees gave little shade. Ruppi and his family walked to a cool resting place in a sandy gully where they all dozed off to sleep.

"Then we heard someone calling, Yai! Yai! Yai!" said Ruppi. "We all stood up and looked around. The four dogs were barking wildly so we knew that strangers were approaching the camp. The old man, my father Gundu, grabbed his boomerangs and spears; he fitted a spear into a woomera and waited.

"I was only a young fella then, I been through the Law but not married yet," said Ruppi. "There was my daddy, two mummies [his father's two wives] and three sisters, but three brothers left months earlier, one to Wiluna, one to Leonora, the eldest stayed in Jigalong," he explained.

The family scanned the dry salt lakes for any signs of movement then they saw them. "I saw them first and shouted out, 'There they are.' They were Mardus, six of them, all men and four dogs. My brother Chummy, the one who moved here to Jigalong earlier, came with them," said Ruppi, pausing to take a sip of cold sweet tea from the billy can, then he continued his story.

"We were happy to see them, especially my brother Barlu." He nodded his head towards a tall, lean middle-aged man who was putting the finishing touches to his spear. The other five men were Mandildjara and Gududjara people from the north-west. Ruppi's people were Budidjara and this was their traditional land.

The visitors brought two cooked emu legs as well as gifts of tea, sugar, flour and tobacco, which were sampled immediately. Everybody was impressed. Ruppi explained that they had looked at their visitors in disbelief when they were told that this was only part of the weekly rations that were distributed by the boss at the Jigalong depot.

That evening, while the group were sitting down around the fire eating their supper, the visitors told them of terrible events that were frightening all the Mardu people throughout the desert.

"They told us about the white men who were using powerful weapons called guns. My daddy told them that he knew what guns were. He had seen them," Ruppi said. "The white men who passed through this part of the salt lakes country had used them to shoot kangaroos and emus for food."

The Budidjara people became very concerned and afraid. They stared silently into the glowing embers until the women got up and walked into the darkness returning a few minutes later dragging more wood behind them. The men rose and returned to their camp to talk "men's business". Their discussions went on well into the night. At last, when all the news from other groups had been gleaned and every piece of family gossip had been shared, the old man Gunbu returned to his spouses and made himself as comfortable as he could on the dry, dusty earth and drifted off to sleep. Ruppi stayed with the visitors and slept near them.

Waking at first light, the old man dusted the red dirt off his bottom and hips then tied his hair belt around his waist and walked some distance from the camp, returning later with more wood for the fire. He raked the embers and tossed on some dry spinifex grass then piled small twigs and the heavier pieces on the top.

"Bukala, bukala," he urged. There was no response so

he repeated the order. "Bukala, bukala." This time everyone heard him and the camp began to stir.

After breakfast of emu, damper and billy tea, Gunbu announced that they were leaving their homelands to settle in Jigalong. The visitors had convinced him that this was the right decision. No one was surprised, the women expected it somehow. Although they weren't driven off their land by the white man, all the men agreed that it was the right thing to do under the circumstances.

"We will be safe there," Gunbu assured his family. "Besides, my boy tells me that there are a few Banaka men and girls waiting to get married. Husbands for my daughters and a wife for my son," he said with an air of satisfaction. He knew that when his family arrived at the depot they would be given gifts of food and tobacco by potential spouses.

The old man stood up clutching his spears, boomerangs and some smaller weapons that he pushed into his hair belt. The other men did the same, making sure that their secret and sacred paraphenalia was hidden out of sight of prying eyes. The women gathered their coolamons and what was left of the food, and a new and most important gift of a canvas water bag, still half filled with water.

"Bukala, bukala," ordered the old man. "We gotta long way to go. We go now," he told them as he faced south-east towards Lake Nabberu along the rabbit-proof fence.

The men took the lead, the women followed behind. The old man took two dogs with him and veered to the left over a small gully to some mulga trees. The women, accompanied by two skinny dogs, moved on. They met up again in the late afternoon and made a huge fire so that the smoke would guide them to the camp. Some fresh meat was cooked in the ashes and a small portion was eaten and the bones and other remains were given to the dogs. The rest was saved for the next day. Although large game was scarce they managed to catch a bush turkey, goannas and a few galahs that rested in the river gums along the banks of the creeks.

When they reached the rabbit-proof fence they followed it to Savory Creek. The journey took several days, starting at sunrise, walking until midday, resting, then continuing until dusk when they would make a camp for the night.

"When we got to Jigalong," said Ruppi "my big brother takes us to his camp on the river bank, close to the rabbit-proof fence."

"After dinner my sister-in-law Minta take us to the store to get 'em midka and jawuja and jaarta and jina-jina for all the women."

That night the new arrivals from the desert were introduced to "civilisation" as they ate the white man's food and wore his hot, uncomfortable clothes. Several days later the women were seen around the camp wearing not one but two or three dresses of varying lengths, colours and patterns. No one thought to tell them to wear one at a time, they were merely instructed on how to wear a frock, and no one explained that when the dress became soiled they must take it off and put on a clean one.

"They tell us we gotta cover everything, the wudgebulla don't like to see neked fullah," said Ruppi. "We never like to put clothes on first time but we had to, we had no choice."

These people who were used to walking around the desert without clothing could not understand why or what covering one's nakedness had to do with the seeking and the acceptance of food and sanctuary. The Mardu also realised that the white strangers were not the only foreigners that they had to adjust to, there were also the large beasts that were thought at first to be marbus but they discovered that these animals were horses. The Aboriginal name given to them was yowada. As well as horses there were other strange imported animals such as cattle, sheep, foxes and rabbits.

The rabbits adapted to this hot arid land immediately and they thrived and multiplied at an alarming rate. In an attempt to control the rabbit population, the rabbit-proof fence was constructed and completed in 1907. In Western Australia the fence covered a distance of 1,834 kilometres and ran from the Southern Ocean near the port of Esperance in the south to the tropical Eighty Mile Beach north of Port Hedland. The government of the day proposed that a properly constructed and a well-maintained fence of barbed wire would halt the invasion of rabbits into Western Australia from the eastern states. But the theory was proved wrong — there were more rabbits on the Western Australian side of the fence than there were on the South Australian side.

At strategic points along the fence small depots were established. Fencing contractors were employed as inspectors to patrol the fence and repair sections that were damaged by flood, fire, emus and kangaroos. They rode on camels or horses in pairs up and down the fence and each pair of riders was responsible for patrolling 240 kilometres.

The rabbit-proof fence became an important landmark to everyone, including the Mardudjara people migrating from the desert regions. Once they reached the rabbit-proof fence they followed it to Jigalong.

Old man Gunbu and his family settled in well at Jigalong. Two of his daughters married Banaka men from the Mandildjara group while their youngest daughter married a Banaka man from the Gudidjara people. One of the women, Minden, had a lovely daughter whom the superintendent called Maude.

Five years after settling at Jigalong, Maude's grandparents died. The old man Gunbu went to bed one night and never woke up again. His first wife Maupi, Maude's grandmother, had a chest infection that was probably influenza, from which she never recovered. Ruppi's mother Duddi, Gunbu's second wife, went to live with her son and daughter-in-law on Balfour Downs Station.

Maude grew up in a warm, loving environment and brought joy and laughter into the lives of many people. She was very small for her age but that didn't stop her from playing with other relations in nearby camps. She proved to them that she could climb the huge river gums along the river as well as anyone.

During the Christmas holidays almost everyone left their usual camps and moved closer to where the "big meetings" were held.

5

Jigalong, 1907–1931

*J*IGALONG WAS established as a government depot in 1907. It was the base for the maintenance men who travelled up and down the rabbit-proof fence, clearing away branches of trees and tumbleweed that may have been blown against the fence or any dead animals that had been caught in the barbed wire. The Superintendent of the depot was also the Protector of Aborigines. At that time the staff at the depot consisted of two white men, the white women arrived later.

Food rations, clothing, tobacco and blankets were distributed amongst the Mardu people who came in from the desert. The depot began to arouse the curiosity and interest of the nomadic people in the area. Small numbers, mainly kinship groups, wandered in to see for themselves what this place had to offer them. The old people were growing tired of the hardships and the constant searching for food since the supply was now scarce. But more importantly, they wanted a refuge, a place where they could sleep safely at night without fear of attack by the white men. The young men were still suspicious and slightly apprehensive but dutifully accompanied their old people.

By the 1930s the numbers at the Jigalong depot had grown steadily as more people came in from the desert.

The elders decided that Jigalong would be their base camp for holding their sacred and secret ceremonies. Sacred objects were brought in from their hiding places in the desert and buried there, thus signifying a permanent "sitting down place". As they came and settled, the people did not abandon their nomadic lifestyle entirely but adapted to one that was semi-nomadic. They remained where the food supply was plentiful and continuous and when they wanted to supplement this regular diet of government rations they went out hunting and gathering the traditional foods. This became a regular weekend event.

A big meeting held during the holidays at the end of the year was a time when all the cultural rituals and ceremonies of traditional significance were performed. The young boys entered the initiation camps and the young girls were formally given to their bilgurs, if they were durn-durns. Like all the other girls, Maude knew who her bilgur was as they had been betrothed when she was a baby. So every year when she attended these meetings with her parents, she was apprehensive and hoped that her time to leave them had not yet come. When the announcement was finally made she and her family were totally unprepared.

"I don't want Maudie as my wife. I want her cousin sister," her bilgur told the meeting. Maude hung her head, she didn't want others to see the relief and pleasure on her face. Her family stood up and yelled abuse at him. She was sixteen at the time and she was glad that she wasn't marrying old Gillbu, although he was a very kind and generous old man. Maude only pretended that she was humiliated by the rejection. She liked things as they were and wished they would never change. She was luckier than most of the girls of her age. When she was about twelve years old, Maude became the first Mardu girl to be trained as a domestic help for Mr Hawkins, the Superintendent at the depot. She was bright and very intelligent and quickly learned to speak the English language. The Superintendent often called on her to act as a translator for newcomers arriving from surrounding areas. She proved to be a happy, reliable worker, and often accompanied her parents back to the claypan where they had made their camp.

Her father, Willabi, and two uncles worked with the gang from the rabbit-proof fence. There had been three different maintenance inspectors since they started; the new man was a good boss and they liked him very much. Sometimes he stayed at their camp to share a meal with Maude's family. He enjoyed the kangaroo stews and dampers that her mother and aunts made. The workers also called in at various times for a hot meal when they were in the area.

One day her mother noticed that the light cotton shift Maude was wearing seemed to be too tight around the stomach. At first she thought it must be all the good tucker she had been eating, but as the days wore on she realised that her only child was expecting a baby. One evening when Willabi returned home from south of the claypan near Lake Nubbera, she mentioned her suspicions to him.

Who was the baby's father they wanted to know. Since her rejection by her betrothed, Maude spent most of her time with them at the depot. Willabi decided to confront their daughter after breakfast before he went to work. They were both relieved to find that Maude had not broken any kinship laws by having a boyfriend from the wrong group. The child's father was none other than the boss himself. His name was Thomas Craig, an Englishman who was employed as an inspector of the rabbit-proof fence for a few years. He was saving enough money to buy a farm in the Lake Grace in the Dumbleyung area.

The family remained at Bunda-Bunda, a claypan south of Jigalong, except for the occasional trips to the depot to pick up food rations and to gather the latest news and gossip. Summer came and went, the cold winds were blowing relentlessly across the salt lakes into the camp. Huge campfires were burning fiercely, the flames leaping in all directions forcing her mother and her two aunts to search for a warm spot out of the range of flames. At first they all stood facing the fire, with their hands spread out in front of them like fans, then turned around to feel the fire's warmth on their backs.

If only the bitterly cold desert winds would stop, sighed Maude. She wasn't feeling well, it must be the emu she had for supper. She told her mother that she had a stomach ache but each time she went to the toilet nothing happened. Her mother and aunts watched her movements very closely.

"The baby, he come soon," one of her aunts said very quietly. The others nodded in agreement.

"Come on girl," urged her mother. "We go and make a camp in the river over there," she said, pointing beyond the mulga trees. "Plenty of worru and soft bunna. Your baby be coming soon," she added softly.

Maude was feeling worse, the terrible pains in her stomach were spreading around her lower back. Meekly and slowly she followed the three older women over the banks of the dry Savory Creek where a wuungku was hastily built. Soon a big fire was lit.

"You lie down on the blankets over there, not too close to the fire," her mother told her.

"Now lay down," said her oldest aunt, "on your back." Between them the two aunts pulled her shift up over her swollen stomach and began massaging it, while her mother watched anxiously. They kept rubbing and touching her stomach and back for what seemed like hours. Then they watched as the uterus dilated to reveal the baby's head.

"It's a wandi, a muda-muda wandi," the aunts told the young mother.

"See," said her Aunt Gauldi, holding the babe so that the grandmother could see her. Then while her sisters began rubbing the warm, dry sand over the child to remove all the amniotic fluid from its body it was customary for the grandmother to protect the baby from any evil spirits who may be lurking nearby.

She began shouting loudly, "Look at this baby, it's the ugliest child I ever saw. She is too ugly to look at, and I know that she will grow up to be a naughty girl." She hurled all sorts of insults about her grandchild to protect her from any possible harm brought by evil spirits who may have witnessed the birth. After the ritual was completed, she stood up.

"You go to sleep, everything's alright now," Aunt Gauldi assured Maude.

The women remained in the creek until the men returned from their work on the rabbit-proof fence. Maude's father and uncles and the white worker were expected back at the camp in a couple of days' time. The boss, the baby's father, was due to return to Jigalong the following week. The baby remained nameless until he arrived, then he called her Molly after his sister.

When Molly was almost six weeks' old Maude took her up to show Mr Keeling, the Superintendent. The child was wrapped in a piece of calico and was sound asleep in her mother's arms. Mr Keeling said all the nice things about the babe and wished them good health and issued Maude with her own ration order, which included a few yards of unbleached calico to make clothes for the baby. He later recorded in his files that he had just seen the first half-caste child to be born amongst the Jigalong people.

Molly grew into a pretty little girl. Her mother was very proud of her and her father brought her gifts of clothing and pretty coloured ribbons. The other members of the family received parcels of brightly coloured material and tobacco. These gifts were shared amongst family members and the community, and were proudly displayed and shown-off to the people at the depot.

As she grew older, Molly often wished that she didn't have light skin so that she didn't have to play by herself. Most of the time she would sit alone, playing in the red dusty flats or in the riverbed depending where her family had set up camp. The dust-covered child stood out amongst her darker playmates. The Mardu children insulted her and said hurtful things about her. Some told her that because she was neither Mardu or wudgebulla she was like a mongrel dog. She reacted in the only way she knew. She grabbed handfuls of sand or stones and threw them at her tormentors, and sometimes she chased them with a stick. After a while she became used to the insults, and although they still hurt she didn't show it. One morning, when Molly was about four years old, her mother told her some exciting news. Two of her aunties had babies, little girls, and they were both muda-mudas like her.

The first question Molly asked was, "When are they coming to Jigalong?" She was very happy. Now she had two sisters.

First came Daisy, who was born at Mad Donkey Well, south-west of Jigalong towards Mundiwindi Station. She was followed by Gracie, who was born at Walgun Station northwest of the depot.

As they grew older, Gracie and Molly became inseperable and they supported each other when other children teased them. They also saw Daisy quite frequently when her family moved closer to work on Murra Munda Station.

Mr Keeling had been taking a great deal of interest in Molly and Gracie. One day while he was observing the children at play, he noticed that the attitude of the Mardu children towards the two girls was unfair. He wrote to the Department of Native Affairs in Perth advising them that the girls would be better off if they were removed from Jigalong. In his report he mentioned that the girls, "were not getting a fair chance as the blacks consider the H/Cs [half-castes] inferior to them ..." (Department of Native Affairs file no. 173/30.)

Thousands of miles south, politicians and other officials

were planning the destinies of children like Molly, Gracie and Daisy.

Official concern shifted from the decreasing numbers of traditional or full-blood Aborigines to the half-castes and part-Aboriginal children who were being born all over the country. The common belief at the time was that part-Aboriginal children were more intelligent than their darker relations and should be isolated and trained to be domestic servants and labourers. Policies were introduced by the government in an effort to improve the welfare and educational needs of these children. Molly, Gracie and Daisy were completely unaware that they were to be included in the schemes designed for children who were fathered by white men. Their mothers were accused of being promiscuous. A few critics were honest, however, when they said many white men satisfied their lustful desires with the native women until they were able to return to white society.

Eventually the Western Australian government decided to establish two institutions for Aboriginal children with white fathers: one at Carralup Settlement near Katanning in the south-west, and the Moore River Native Settlement, north of Perth and 13 kilometres west of Mogumber. Although the births of these children were not registered they were still noted by station owners in their journals so it was easy for the authorities to locate them. Also, movement between stations throughout the Pilbara was not quite as frequent then as it is today because the travel was mostly by foot. This helped the government officials to track down a family group.

Patrol officers travelled far and wide removing part-Aboriginal children from their families and transported them hundreds of kilometres down south. Every mother of a part-Aboriginal child was aware that their offspring could be taken away from them at any time and they were powerless to stop the abductors. That is why many women preferred to give birth in the bush rather than in a hospital where they believed their babies would be taken from them soon after birth.

The years passed by and the seasons came and went. Except for a couple of years of severe drought when no rain was recorded in the district, nothing extraordinary happened — life and the cycle of nature proceeded. Molly, Gracie and Daisy had outgrown the insults and the teasings. Once the other children accepted their differences, their lives became quite normal. Nevertheless, the trio stood out from the main community at the depot.

No matter where the three girls went, there was always someone watching them very closely and recording their behaviour just as Mrs Chellow from Murra Munda Station did on 9 December 1930 when she wrote to the Commissioner of Native Affairs.

Murra Munda
9th December 1930

Mr Neville
Chief Protector of Aborigines,
PERTH

… There are two half-caste girls at Jigalong — Molly 15 years, Crissy [also called Gracie] 11 years; in my opinion I think you should see about them as they are running wild with the whites.

(Sgd) Mrs Chellow.
(Department of Native Affairs File No. 175/30)

The girls were very fortunate to be part of a loving, caring family who tried to compensate for all the nasty insults and abuse by spoiling and indulging them at home. Their grandfather even went as far as to take them on walkabouts in the bush where he ground black charcoal into fine powder and rubbed it into their bodies, covering them from their faces right down to their toes. This powder, he promised, would solve all their problems. It would darken their light skins and end all the teasings and tauntings, but most importantly, it would protect them and prevent them from being taken away from their families. The trio was joined by ever-increasing numbers of half-caste or part-Aboriginal children in the East Pilbara region. However, the birth rate there was insignificant compared to the rate in the south-west of the state.

In July 1930, the rainy season was exceptionally good. For the Mardu people throughout the Western Desert this was the season for taking long walks in the bush, foraging for bush tucker and feasting on the day's catch. Every Mardu welcomes the glorious warm weather, when the azure skies are even bluer against the grey-green mulga trees and the red dusty earth; grass grows under the small shrubs and between the sandy patches around the rocky ledges and even the spinifex is fresh and green. Alas, like everything that is revived and resurrected by the winter rains their beauty and brilliance is shortlived. They seem to fade and die so quickly.

Molly and Gracie spent a lovely weekend with their families digging for kulgu yams and collecting bunches of yellow flowers from the desert oaks, which they brought home to share with those who stayed behind to take care of the old people and the dogs. They soaked bunches of flowers in a bucket of water to make a sweet, refreshing drink. The other bush foods, such as the girdi girdi, murrandus and bush turkeys, were shared amongst the community. After supper the weary girls curled up in their swags and in no time at all, they were fast asleep.

Early next morning, Molly's step-father Galli rose at dawn and lit the fire. He made a billy of tea and sat under the shade of a large river gum, drinking a mug of warm tea. He glanced over to the sleeping forms of his two wives, and called out, "Come on, get up." The women began to stir. Galli then cut a piece of plug tobacco and crushed it in his hand, mixed the pure white ashes of the leaves of the mulga tree into it then put it into his mouth and began to chew the gulja, spitting the juice occasionally. In the old days, the people would collect and chew the leaves of wild or bush tobacco that grew on the cliffs or on rock ledges.

The Mardus preferred the white man's tobacco, plug tobacco, because it was easily available and also it was stronger and lasted longer. They chewed it and spat out the juice, the same way that other races chewed betel leaves.

Maude was Galli's second wife. She and his other wife both belonged to the same group under the kinship system. Both were Garimaras, the spouse category for Galli. Between them they prepared breakfast for the whole family, which included three big dampers cooked in the hot ashes of the fire and the girdi girdi leftover from the hunting trip in the bush. They all agreed that it had been a successful and enjoyable day.

Molly and Daisy finished their breakfast and decided to take all their dirty clothes and wash them in the soak further down the river. They returned to the camp looking clean and refreshed and joined the rest of the family in the shade for lunch of tinned corned beef, damper and tea. The family had just finished eating when all the camp dogs began barking, making a terrible din.

"Shut up," yelled their owners, throwing stones at them. The dogs whinged and skulked away.

Then all eyes turned to the cause of the commotion. A tall, rugged white man stood on the bank above them. He could easily have been mistaken for a pastoralist or a grazier with his tanned complexion except that he was wearing khaki clothing. Fear and anxiety swept over them when they realised that the fateful day they had been dreading had come at last. They always knew that it would only be a matter of time before the government would track them down. When Constable Riggs, Protector of Aborigines, finally spoke his voice was full of authority and purpose. They knew without a doubt that he was the one who took their children in broad daylight — not like the evil spirits who came into their camps in the night.

"I've come to take Molly, Gracie and Daisy, the three half-caste girls, with me to go to school at the Moore River Native Settlement," he informed the family.

The old man nodded to show that he understood what Riggs was saying. The rest of the family just hung their heads refusing to face the man who was taking their daughters away from them. Silent tears welled in their eyes and trickled down their cheeks.

"Come on, you girls," he ordered. "Don't worry about taking anything. We'll pick up what you need later."

When the two girls stood up, he noticed that the third girl was missing. "Where's the other one, Daisy?" he asked anxiously.

"She's with her mummy and daddy at Murra Munda Station," the old man informed him.

"She's not at Murra Munda or at Jimbalbar goldfields. I called into those places before I came here," said the Constable. "Hurry up then, I want to get started. We've got a long way to go yet. You girls can ride this horse back to the depot," he said, handing the reins over to Molly. Riggs was annoyed that he had to go miles out of his way to find these girls.

Molly and Gracie sat silently on the horse, tears streaming down their cheeks as Constable Riggs turned the big bay stallion and led the way back to the depot. A high pitched wail broke out. The cries of agonised mothers and the women, and the deep sobs of grandfathers, uncles and cousins filled the air. Molly and Gracie looked back just once before they disappeared through the river gums. Behind them, those remaining in the camp found strong sharp objects and gashed themselves and inflicted wounds to their heads and bodies as an expression of their sorrow.

The two frightened and miserable girls began to cry, silently at first, then uncontrollably; their grief made worse by the lamentations of their loved ones and the visions of them sitting on the ground in their camp letting their tears mix with the red blood that flowed from the cuts on their heads. This reaction to their children's abduction showed that the family were now in mourning. They were grieving for their abducted children and their relief would come only when the tears ceased to fall, and that will be a long time yet.

At the depot, Molly and Gracie slid down from the horse and followed Constable Riggs to the car.

Mr Hungerford, the Superintendent, stopped them and spoke to Riggs.

"While you are here, there's a native woman with a fractured thigh, in the other natives' camp, the one on the banks of the river. Can you take a look at her, Constable?"

"Yes, I'll examine her," replied the Constable.

"I'll come with you," said Hungerford. "We'll borrow that native boy Tommy's horse and sulky," he added. "I'll fix him up with some rations later as payment."

After Riggs had splinted the woman's leg, he told Hungerford that he would have to take her back with him to the Marble Bar Hospital. "Lift her gently onto the sulky," he asked her two brothers who were standing watch nearby.

As Hungerford seated himself beside Constable Riggs he said, "And by the way, the other woman, Nellie arrived from Watchtower Station while you were collecting Molly and Gracie. You know the one suffering from VD. She needs to go to the hospital too."

"Alright," Riggs replied. "But I still intend to speak to

Frank Matthews, the station manager about her and remind him that he has no right to examine or treat any of the natives here. That should be left to us. We are the Protectors of Aborigines in this district."

Constable Rigg was referring to the Protection Policy Regulation, number 106m:

Whenever a native falls ill, becomes diseased or sustains an accident and such illness, disease or accident appears to an employer to require medical attention or hospital treatment beyond that which can be efficiently or reasonably given at the place of employment, the employer shall as soon as reasonably possible, send the native to the nearest or most accessible hospital or to the nearest protector and thence to the nearest and most, accessible hospital at the protectors discretion.

The crippled woman, Mimi-Ali, was transferred from the sulky to the car with Molly and Gracie.

"Tommy," yelled Constable Riggs. "Take your horse and sulky to Walgun Station and wait for me there," he ordered.

"Molly and Gracie, you had better sit in front with me, and you Nellie, can sit in the back with Mimi-Ali," said Riggs as he cranked the car.

Half an hour later he was greeted by Matthews. "You have a load this time, Constable Riggs," he said as the officer got out of the car.

"Yes, I know. It can't be helped. I've got the two sick native women. Which reminds me, there is something I must speak to you about."

The Constable explained the duties of the Protectors of Aborigines in the Nullagine district and cautioned Matthews that he should not take on those responsibilities himself.

"I'd better get moving," said Constable Riggs. "I have to search around for Daisy. I'll call in next time I'm on patrol in the district."

The patrol officer drew up in front of the Walgun Homestead gate and was greeted by Mr and Mrs Cartwright, managers of the station.

"Hello," said Don Cartwright as he shook hands with the visitor.

"Come inside and have a cuppa tea," said his wife warmly, pointing towards the door.

"Thank you, but not just yet. I must find the half-caste girl, Daisy," he said. "She's somewhere between here and Murra Munda Station, near the soak. I already have the other two, Molly and Gracie in the car with Mimi-Ali from Jigalong and Nellie, the cook from Watchtower Station who are in need of medical attention."

"But where are you taking those half-caste girls?" asked Mrs Cartwright.

"They're going south to the Moore River Native Settlement, where we hope they will grow up with a better outlook on life than back at their camp," he answered with great satisfaction.

"I'll leave the car here but first I'll drop the women off at the native workers' camp. I'll take Molly and Gracie with me, though," he said. "I don't want them to clear out."

Constable Riggs drove slowly down to the camp, followed closely by Tommy with his horse and sulky. Soon, he and Tommy were heading across the flats, over the spinifex grass and through the mulga trees in search of Daisy, who was with her family at the camp. Finding her had proved more difficult than the Constable expected. He had searched the Jimbalbar and Murra Munda area on horseback covering 60 kilometres, and a further 30 kilometres in the dry, rough country between Murra Munda and Walgun stations before he finally found her. The search was so tiring that he decided to spend the night at Walgun Station. His passengers stayed at the camp with Gracie's mother Lilly, her grandmother, Frinda, and some other relatives.

At 3.30 in the morning, on 16 July, the Constable noticed that rain was threatening. The roads were bad enough as it was, but when wet they were even more hazardous so he decided to make a start.

"I don't want to be marooned on the road with these natives," Constable Riggs explained to the Cartwrights.

"We understand," said Mrs Cartwright, "we'll see you when you're in the district. Have a safe trip home."

"Thank you. I'd better get going," he said. "The women must have finished their breakfast by now, so I'll go down and pick them up. Thanks again for your hospitality."

Grace's mother, old Granny Frinda and other relations in the camp began to wail and cry.

"Worrah, Worrah! He take 'em way, my grannies [grand-daughters], wailed the old lady, as she bent down with great difficulty and picked up a billy can and brought it down heavily on her head. She and the rest of the women began to wail louder, their hearts now burdened with sadness of the girls' departure and the uncertainty of ever seeing them again. The girls were also weeping. The wailing grew louder as the vehicle that was taking them away headed towards the gate. Each girl felt the pain of being torn from their mothers' and grandmothers' arms.

As the car disappeared down the road, old Granny Frinda lay crumpled on the red dirt calling for her grand-daughters and cursing the people responsible for their abduction. In their grief the women asked why their children should be taken from them. Their anguished cries echoed across the flats, carried by the wind. But no one listened to them, no one heard them.

A couple of hours after the three girls had been driven away, Gracie's mother, distraught and angry, was still sitting on the ground rocking back and forth. Maude and her brother-in-law had ridden over in a horse and cart to discuss the distressing news and stayed to comfort and support each other. Some time later, she calmed down enough to hurl a mouth full of abuse at Alf Fields, Gracie's white father, who was standing silently near the galvanised iron tank. She screamed at him in Aboriginal English and Mardu wangku, and beat his chest with her small fists.

"Why didn't you stop them?" she cried out in anger and frustration.

"I couldn't stop them taking my daughter — yes, she is my daughter too," he said sadly. He was so proud of his beautiful black-haired daughter whom he had named after his idol, English singer Gracie Fields.

He tried to explain to her mother that the patrol officer was a government representative and an officer of the Crown. Had he interfered or tried to stop the man he would have been arrested and put in gaol and charged with obstructing the course of justice. Gracie's mother didn't listen.

"You are a white man too, they will listen to you. Go and talk to them," she pleaded softly.

"I am sorry but I can't do anything to stop them taking our daughter away from us," he said finally.

She couldn't accept his excuse or forgive him for just standing by and doing nothing to prevent their daughter from being taken away from them. She packed up and moved to Wiluna.

6

The Journey South

*T*HE THREE GIRLS were not used to rising before dawn so they settled down in the car and fell asleep. When they opened their eyes they realised that they had slept longer than they expected. They had passed through Ethel Creek and Roy Hill stations and were on the main road to Nullagine, which was an unsealed dirt track, full of pot holes and fine red bull dust that seemed to fill the car.

They were so exhausted they couldn't cry anymore and they spoke only in whispers and sign language.

Except for a curt, "You girls awright back there!" the policeman didn't speak to them or tell the girls where he was taking them. All they knew was that they were going to the settlement to go to school. The rain clouds were gathering and by the time they reached the bend where large grey boulders loomed above on either side of the road, the sky was black with rain clouds. Riggs glanced up at the dark clouds, while his passengers in the back sat silently watching the landscape change as they passed through it. They paid no attention to the beautiful scenery or the long shadows of the tall river gums. Their interest was aroused only when they saw animals such as kangaroos, emus, horses and camels. Otherwise, they sat quite still until one nudged the other to look at something as they passed by.

In his role as a Protector of Aborigines, Constable Riggs had been on the move for over a week and would have completed the round trip when he arrived at Marble Bar. Except for a brief pause at stations along the way they spent most of the day driving. At 2 o'clock they arrived at Marble Bar hospital where Riggs admitted the sick women, then he handed Molly, Gracie and Daisy to Constable Melrose for removal south.

Constable Riggs returned to Nullagine at 5 pm the same day. With great relief and satisfaction he notified the Chief Protector of Aborigines in Perth by telegram. "All half-castes and sick natives transported Bar train tomorrow report earliest. Riggs Const." 21 July 1931.

It was late afternoon when the party reached Marble Bar. When they arrived, Constable Melrose handed Molly, Gracie and Daisy over to his wife as he had to visit the local Aboriginal camp to attend to a young girl who was sick and had to be taken into the Marble Bar hospital.

"Feed them an early supper and I'll lock them up in the empty cells," Melrose told his wife. "I want a good night's sleep tonight."

And so while Mimi-Ali and Nellie were resting at the Marble Bar hospital, Molly, Gracie and Daisy spent the next few days at the Marble Bar police station under the supervision of Constable Melrose. Nellie remained in hospital when the others later boarded the train under the escort of Constable Pollett to Port Hedland. Travelling by train was much better than by car but Molly, Gracie and Daisy were growing weary. The girls knew that they had left behind the rugged landscape of the East Pilbara when they sighted the blue-green ocean. They were fascinated by the beauty of the sea, but had no idea what they were doing there until they drove down to the wharf and were handed over to the captain of the State Shipping Service vessel the *Koolinda*. It was berthed at the harbour waiting for high tide. After Constable Pollett handed over the documents to the captain, he turned towards the nervous young girls and told them that the captain would be taking them all the way to Fremantle.

Captain Freeman called to a member of the crew, Gwen Campbell, the stewardess. "Here's another four for you. There's Molly, Daisy, Gracie and the woman with the fractured femur is Mimi-Ali. Take them down to their cabins," he said.

Campbell asked the girls to follow her to the lower deck while another crew member carried Mimi-Ali in a stretcher. So, on the 26 July 1931, Molly, Daisy, Gracie and Mimi-Ali sailed south to the Port of Fremantle. A telegram was sent to Chief Protector of Aborigines in Perth. "Half-caste girls Daisy Mollie and Gracie and crippled gin Ballerallie [Mimi-Ali] from Marble Bar forwarded *Koolinda* last night care stewardess stop please arrange meet and have stretcher for Ballerallie. Pollett Constable." 27 July 1931.

As the vessel chugged slowly out into the the deep, blue

| "FOR QUICK SERVICE USE THE TELEGRAPH" THE INFORMATION ON THE BACK OF THIS FORM WILL INTEREST YOU | COMMONWEALTH OF AUSTRALIA—POSTMASTER-GENERAL'S DEPARTMENT. **RECEIVED TELEGRAM.** The first line of this telegram contains the following particulars in the order named. | T.G. 40 OFFICE DATE STAMP |

RECEIVED TELEGRAM.

Station From.   Words.   Time Lodged.   No.

PT HEDLAND   . 33   9 15 AM

To   COLLECT   2/5
ABDEPT   6.
PERTH

27 JULY 193

HALFCASTE GIRLS DAISY MOLLIE AND GRACE AND CRIPPLED GIN
BALLERALLIE FROM MARBLE BAR FORWARDED KOOLINDA LAST NIGHT
CARE STEWARDESS STOP PLEASE ARRANGE MEET AND HAVE STRETCHER
FOR BALLERALLIE   POLLETT CONSTABLE   10 16 AM TC

Mimi Hi

waters of the open sea, the three girls anxiously clutched their bunks, overcome with fear. They let themselves roll from side to side until they got used to the grinding and murmuring of the ship's engines. Then they stretched out on their bunks and went to sleep.

The next morning after breakfast, Gwen Campbell coaxed them out on deck. "Come and see all the big fish," she said, as she beckoned them to her. "We may be able to throw a line over this afternoon and catch some for supper."

They stood near the railing and watched as the mulloway, schnapper, kingfish and many other types of fish darted this way and that in the ocean below them.

As the days wore on Gwen Campbell tried gently to gain their trust but they remained shy and frightened. George Johnson, a crew member, told them of the exciting and fascinating places he had visited. He spoke of the pyramids of Egypt and how these unusual burial places were built by slaves.

"Slave people?" they wanted to ask him. "Are they like us or the same as you?" But they were too timid.

George told them about the many races of people in the world. The girls liked to listen to his tales about the countries that he had visited and also about the places that he would like to see. Sometimes he and Gwen encouraged the three youngsters to go for a stroll on deck in the evening, while it was pleasant and warm. They were good sailors, George told them. During their evening walks he taught them the English names for the stars. On calm nights he would tell them to look to the night skies.

"Look over there. That's the Southern Cross," he would say. "If you are ever lost in the bush, let it be your guide. If it's a clear night, look for it. Remember, the Southern Cross is found in the south-west of the dark sky.

"And there's the Big Dipper, see up there," he said, pointing to the thousands of twinkling stars. The girls saw it but said nothing. They just nodded silently.

"Now, it's off to bed you go. In a couple of day's time we'll berth at Fremantle," Gwen told them, as she escorted them back to their cabins. "Good night," she said and she closed the door. "I'll see you tomorrow."

The girls didn't see George the next morning, he was on early shift. Raymond Baxter was escorting them instead. "Gwen is busy with other passengers. She'll come down later," he explained.

Raymond was a lanky sailor with red hair and freckles all over his face. His bright blue eyes twinkled as he laughed and yakked with the others. He wasn't as old as his friend George but they liked him as well. They were all leaning against the rail around the deck when Raymond shouted excitedly, "Look over there. Porpoises." Porpoises, thought the girls from the Western Desert, what are they? As if reading their minds the red haired sailor explained, "They are the smallest species of dolphins. You see them in all the oceans of the world."

The girls watched with great interest as the six graceful mammals sailed into the air and nose dived smoothly into the turquoise ocean.

The porpoises lept up in pairs as if the movements were

choreographed by some unknown being. The girls stood mesmerised while the ship rose and fell as the huge waves swelled and heaved beneath them and they watched until the beautiful creatures were out of sight.

"It looks like we're in for wet weather," said Raymond, breaking the magic spell. "The clouds seem to be building up in the west." Just as he finished there was a roll of thunder followed by a flash of lightning.

"Yes, we're in for a wet night. You'd better go back into your cabin. Come on then," he said.

They settled back in their cosy, warm cabin, and "read" comics that the sailor had given them. Although none of the girls could read, they looked at the pretty illustrations and tried to guess what the pictures were saying. The sea was getting very rough and they were beginning to feel frightened and worried. What if this ship tipped over with too much water! They might get drowned. But the stewardess Gwen, supported by Raymond, reassured them that the *Koolinda* was a big, safe ship and certainly would not sink.

"You all go to sleep now. It will be better in the morning. The worst part of the storm will be over," Gwen told them.

The three girls and Mimi-Ali, all from the rugged Pilbara region, had a most pleasant experience sailing down the coast of Western Australia. The weather was sunny and warm from Port Hedland to Geraldton but the further south they sailed the colder and wetter it became. The winds were strong and cold, and the rain made it impossible to stroll on the decks of the ship. Even the beautiful blue-green ocean was changing as they neared the outer reefs of Fremantle Harbour. It turned a dark green colour and the dull grey sky seemed to be reflected on the rough, choppy sea. But as they drew closer to the harbour there was a break in the weather, patches of blue appeared between the grey clouds.

After breakfast of scrambled eggs, toast and sweet, hot tea, George Johnson led the way up to the wet deck for the last time.

"We're nearly there. See over there," he said, pointing to the coast. "That's Fremantle."

The small sailor leant on the rail, puffing his pipe. As the ship sailed closer to the shore he removed the pipe to explain what was to happen next. "Here's the tug boat, the tug master will come on board and take us into port."

They watched with interest and curiosity as the tug drew alongside the *Koolinda* to allow the tug master to transfer from his small boat to sail the ship through the reefs to the safe shipping lane.

"That man knows these waters like the back of his hands, and he'll guide us through the channel to dock safely in the harbour," said George.

"Ah, there are the wheat silos and do you see the other building north of it, the one with the big dingo on the tower?" he asked. "Well, that's where all the flour is made. That's where they grind the wheat that is stored in the silos. They send bags of flour all over the place."

As the red dingo became more visible, Molly, Daisy and Gracie felt an acute pang of homesickness. How many ration bags had their mothers, grandmothers and aunts used with that red dingo — midgi-midgi dgundu — on them? Scores and scores when you think of all the dampers they cooked. When the bags were empty the women made them into bags for carrying food and other items or filled them with old rags and used them as pillows. Bloomers and shifts were also cut out of the flour bags. Yes, they had grown up with the red dingo. Tears welled in their eyes as they remembered their families.

Gwen Campbell's soft voice brought them back to reality. "Come on girls, get your belongings and I'll take you all ashore with me. Eh, by the way, you will need these," she said, as she handed them gaberdine raincoats, which she advised them to put on right away, and a comb and a mirror each. These they put in their calico bags.

After five days of sailing down the coast of Western Australia, they arrived at the Port of Fremantle.

Ten minutes later the girls were following the friendly stewardess without any hesitation down the gangplank and were very relieved when their feet touched the strong timber wharf. They were totally unprepared for the sights and sounds that greeted them. The atmosphere and activity of the busiest seaport in the state was overwhelming and frightening. They huddled closer to the stewardess, seeking her protection. Men were rushing about and yelling; some were watching the cargo being lowered down onto the wharf by huge winches. There were hundreds of bales of wool and crates of dairy produce waiting to be loaded onto ships for export overseas. The girls had never seen so many white men in the one place before. They were very pleased when Gwen Campbell finally said to them, "Here's someone now, see over there."

Matron Campbell (no relation to the stewardess) from the East Perth Girls Home — now the Jack Davis Hostel — waited quietly near the ambulance for the officers to bring Mimi-Ali down the gangplank and for the stewardess to hand over the three girls from Jigalong. Gwen Campbell greeted the Matron cordially. "There are four of them this time," she told her. The ship's crew had done this quite often during the past twelve months.

Matron Campbell said that the Department of Native Affairs had already been advised of the girls' removal from Nullagine so she was expecting them. After delivering the three very shy girls, Gwen Campbell returned to the ship to continue her other regular duties on board. Matron Campbell led them to the ambulance that was waiting to transfer Mimi-Ali to the Royal Perth Hospital. All three climbed in the back and sat on the stretcher beds and waited.

The drive from Fremantle to Perth was comfortable and

interesting. The moment they left the wharf they changed from shy, confused girls to curious, young tourists, interested and amazed at everything they saw, which was all new and different to them.

From their seat in the back of the ambulance, they had a view of the choppy, murky, brown Swan River. Then, as they cruised down Mounts Bay Road, along Riverside Drive, and turned into the bright, lively city, the girls saw hundreds of men wearing suits of brown, grey and navy blue, and each of them wearing hats or caps. There weren't too many women strolling or shopping around town. The few they saw were escorted by men.

It was over a century since the foundation of Western Australia and Perth was now a bustling, thriving capital. There were industrial and commercial buildings everywhere and two and even three-storey department stores and offices. While the girls were staring up at the buildings, a tram trundled noisily past them. It caught them unawares and they jumped back with fright.

"That's a tram. People pay to ride on them," the Matron explained, bemused at the startled looks on her charges' faces.

There were so many cars and trucks coming and going in this big place. It was too mad for the girls. They knew that they could easily get lost in this man-made environment with so few trees and only small patches of bush. To them the city was a noisy and unfriendly place, they didn't like it one bit so they were glad to arrive at the East Perth Girls Home. The Matron led them through the gate and knocked on the front door. It was opened immediately by the cook.

"Eh, come in," she beamed cheerfully. "You are just in time for morning tea," she added as she ushered them into the dining room.

"I am Mrs McKay," said a tall, neat, slim lady. "Come and sit down and tell me your names." Her friendly manner helped the girls to relax while they waited for the tea. The delicious smell of baked fruit scones filled the air.

"You'll join us, won't you Miss Campbell?" Mrs McKay asked the officer.

"Yes, thank you. I have time for a quick cuppa," she replied, sitting down at the large dining table. She couldn't resist the tempting aroma of the scones.

The girls from the remote outback of Western Australia sat nervously as the tea and scones were served. They had never shared a meal with a white woman before so they waited until Mrs McKay coaxed them to join in.

"Come on, don't be shy, eat up, then you can freshen up and have a rest," she said warmly.

Miss Campbell stood and thanked Mrs McKay for the morning tea. Before she left she turned to the girls, there were four of them now, a girl from Moora named Rosie had joined them.

"I'll be picking you up in the morning to take you all to Moore River, so be ready," she said.

The girls began to clear the table when two very attractive sixteen or seventeen-year-old girls came giggling into the room and dumped large paper bags of groceries on the table.

"I am Nora Graham from Sandstone, a mining town in the Murchinson, up near Mt Magnet way," said a short, plump girl with short dark brown curly hair. "I am waiting for a job on a station anywhere around there."

"And I'm Eva Jones from Halls Creek. My father is a prospector there. He was the one who sent me down here to go to school," she said proudly. "He's coming to pick me up soon to take me home," she added. Her eyes sparkled as she thought of him and all the other members of her family in the Kimberley waiting for her return. The four youngsters introduced themselves.

"We only come down to go to school at the settlement

too, then they will send us back to Jigalong," said Molly convincingly.

But what none of these girls realised was that their fate had already been decided by their new guardians, the Commissioners of the Native Affairs Department. Sadly, in only a couple of weeks from then, Nora and Eva would find that instead of returning north as they hoped, they would be sent further south to work as domestics on dairy farms. This would also be their introduction to exploitation and deception; a hard step along the path of life that would have so many twists and turns. As for returning home to their loved ones, well, that would not happen for many, many years.

It was almost nine o'clock when Matron Campbell arrived the next morning to pick up the four girls. Molly, Daisy and Gracie sat in the back seat while Rosie hopped in the front. They sat still and waited for Miss Campbell, and to begin their journey north. Their uneasiness disappeared when they realised that the view from the car window was quite pleasant once they left the city. The landscape changed regularly as they drove along.

The girls from the edge of the desert were fascinated by the lush green pastures and bracken that grew thick and high beside the road. Molly, Daisy and Gracie nudged each other when they saw something that captured their interest, like the majestic red gum trees, the lakes and the herds of dairy cows and flocks of sheep. They pointed at the lakes that were filled with water.

A few hours later, Miss Campbell pulled up under a huge marri gum tree opposite the Mogumber Hotel and went inside. She returned with sandwiches and lemonade for the four girls.

"There you are," she said. "Pass these around. The road is fairly safe so we shouldn't have any trouble from here to the settlement," she told them as she started the car.

The next stop would be their final destination — the

Moore River Native Settlement — the place that the three girls from Jigalong had travelled hundreds of kilometres to reach. It was intended that this would be their home for several years, and where they would be educated in European ways.

Only twelve months before this, Mr A.J. Keeling, the Superintendent at the Government Depot at Jigalong, wrote in his report that, "these children lean more towards the black than white and on second thoughts, think nothing would be gained in removing them". (Department of Native Affairs file no. 173/30.) Someone read it. No one responded.

In a letter dated 4 August 1931, to Constable Riggs, the Chief Protector of Aborigines advised him that,

> the three girls and Mimi-Ali arrived safely, and were met by Matron Campbell of this Department, the party being taken to Perth in the ambulance with Mimi-Ali. The latter is now safely installed at the Perth Hospital, and the girls Daisy, Molly and Chrissy [Gracie] at Moore River Native Settlement. The girls seemed to be very scared of the other children, and required watching to prevent them from running away. We have experienced this condition of mind before, and have always found that they soon accept the inevitable and fall in with the usage of the place.

(Department of Native Affairs file no. 173/30)

7

The Moore River Native Settlement, 1931

*T*HE ROAD OUT to the settlement was almost totally underwater. This made the trip laborious and stressful. The engine strained as the car swayed from side to side and the wheels slid over the muddy road.

"There have been scattered showers all day," Matron Campbell told the girls as they peered anxiously through the windows. "You'd better pull the blankets over your legs," she said, glancing at the thunder clouds rollings over in the west. "It's going to pour down with rain soon." She was worried but there were enough of them to push the car if it got bogged in the soft, clay road.

The trip had taken longer than usual and it was almost dark when they arrived at the settlement. The place was shrouded in fine misty rain and lit only by lights in the centre of the compound. Miss Campbell parked near the staff quarters and the girls waited in the car while she went inside.

"Where's everybody?" whispered Gracie, as she leant closer to the window.

"I don't know," replied Molly softly, glancing curiously around her.

She expected to see at least some of the residents but there was no one about, the whole place seemed to be deserted. Miss Campbell emerged from the stone and lattice staff quarters with another woman.

"These three," she said, pointing to Molly, Daisy and Gracie, "came all the way from Nullagine." The three looked at each other silently. They wanted to tell these midgerji that their home is Jigalong not Nullagine.

"The other one, Rosie, comes from Moora," Miss Campbell said as she handed over to the woman. Then she disappeared behind the trellised building.

"Come with me," said Miss Evans. "I'll take you to your dormitory. This way."

They followed her through the slushy compound to a wooden building. As they approached they noticed that the door was locked with chains and padlocks. Molly saw that the uninviting weatherboard and latticed dormitory had bars on the windows as well. Just like a gaol, she thought, and she didn't like it one bit. The four girls stood around in the cold, their arms folded across their chests trying desperately to control the shivering. They were glad when Miss Evans undid the padlocks, opened the door and invited them to follow her into the already overcrowded dormitory. There were beds everywhere.

"These are your beds, you can choose whichever one you'd like to sleep in. You can please yourself, alright," she said as she turned to leave. She paused, then added, "Eh, I nearly forgot to tell you about the lavatory. Use one of those buckets in the bathroom," she said. "See over there."

Four heads turned in the direction which the woman was pointing but she didn't wait for confirmation, she was anxious to return to her comfortable room next door, behind the white-washed stone wall.

Molly, Daisy and Gracie selected the three beds nearest

to them while Rosie took the one at the other end. The girls found it very difficult to sleep on the hard mattress. They lay feeling cold and lonely, listening to the rain falling on the tin roof. Gracie could stand it no longer, she sneaked quietly to Molly's bed. "Dgudu, I can't sleep," she whispered. "I'm cold. I've only got one rug."

"I am cold too, so bring your rug over here and sleep in my bed," Molly told her shivering young sister.

As Gracie snatched up her rugs Daisy sat up and whispered, "I'm cold too, Dgudu."

"You can sleep jina side," Molly told Daisy, who was already throwing her blanket across the bed.

So, for the rest of the night the three of them cuddled up in the single bed. Very early the next morning they were awakened with a start by a strange voice yelling loudly, "Come on, girls, wakey! wakey! Rise and shine."

The woman went to the first bed and pulled the blankets off the child's head and shook her vigorously then moved on to the next bed and repeated the performance. The new girls were surprised to see the same small, slim woman who had escorted them last night, rushing around peeling the warm rugs from the sleeping children, who mumbled angrily as they were forced to stumble out onto the cold wooden floor. This was a ritual that Miss Evans, the staff member in charge of the dormitories, conducted every morning without fail.

When she came to Molly's bed she stared at the three girls who were now sitting on top of the bed. "Eh, yes, you are the new arrivals. There are four of you, isn't there? Alright, you all make your beds, then go up and have some breakfast at the dining hall. One of the others will show you where it is."

Molly, Daisy and Gracie were able to observe their surroundings and dorm mates more closely in the morning light. They saw that the other girls were just as curious as they were.

"Where are you lot from?" they wanted to know.

"We come from Jigalong," Molly answered without hesitation.

"Where's that?" asked someone from the other end of the dorm.

"Up north," said Molly quietly, she didn't want to say too much to these strangers. She was glad when one of them came over to tell them that she would take them and show them around later.

"But you'd better make your beds first," she said. This was easy, you just straightened the blanket over the mattress. There were no sheets on the beds. They were stored away to be issued only on special occasions to impress special visitors.

"I am Martha Jones. I'm from Port Hedland," said this friendly girl who had volunteered to be their guide. "I've been here for one year now. I came from a station to go to school, then the government gunna send me back to my family to work for the station," she said proudly.

She must have been about fifteen but there was no way of verifying that because, like so many others at the settlement, her birth wasn't registered. The trio from Jigalong liked her instantly. She was a treasure, full of information about everything concerning the settlement and what they could expect while they lived there.

"It's not bad once you get used to things here," Martha told them. The four girls had their doubts about that but said nothing.

The sound of the dining room bell cut short any further conversation. Everyone stood up, patted their beds smooth then headed for the narrow wooden door.

"Come on, we'd better hurry up or we'll end up with cold breakfast," said Martha, leading the way outside. In single file they trailed behind her into the wet, drizzly morning to have their first meal in confined conditions.

Opposite the girls' dormitory, the boys were teeming out

of their own quarters and were making their way over the slushy compound to join the girls for breakfast. This was usually a plate of weevily porridge, bread and dripping washed down by a mug or a tin of lukewarm, sweet, milky tea. All inmates of the compound had their meals in the communal dining room. Like breakfast, the other meals were the most unappealing fare ever served to any human being. Offal collected from the slaughterhouse and taken down to be cleaned and cooked on the coals of a big fire lit on the banks of the river, was more tasty than what was provided by the cook and staff at the kitchen.

After breakfast Martha Jones escorted them outside.

"Eh look, it might fine up later," she said with cheerful optimism as they descended the wooden stairs onto the wet gravelled path that led back to the dormitory. Just as Martha was about to open the door one of the older boys called out to her.

"That's my cousin-brother Bill," she explained. "Our mothers are sisters." The girls from Jigalong understood, as they were also daughters of sisters.

"Go inside and wait for me," she told the four nervous new girls. They weren't sure whether to go inside or wait for her outside. They watched as she started to run but stopped suddenly because she found that the ground was not only slushy but very slippery. Her bare feet made a squelching noise as the mud seeped between her toes. The two cousins met in the middle of the compound and stood talking softly for a few minutes, then parted. While they were waiting for Martha to come in, Molly, Daisy and Gracie whispered in Mardu wangka, their own language.

"I don't like this place," whispered Molly. "It's like a gaol. They lock you up at night time and come and open the door in the morning." They had all noticed the bars across the windows and were really scared of them.

Martha returned to the dormitory and sat on one of the beds near the girls. They were able to have a really good look at their new friend. She was a very pretty girl with short cropped, straight black hair and hazel eyes, but best of all she had a beautiful sparkling smile that made you feel good.

"Bill just wanted to know who you all were and where you came from," Martha said. "He will pass the information on to the rest of them." New arrivals always created great interest but most importantly hope. Hope of news about relations back home.

The rest of the morning was spent in the dormitory sharing information and stories. After lunch the weather had fined up but there were strong gusts of wind blowing across the compound and it was beginning to feel quite cold. Martha Jones suggested they go for their walk. She stood up, gave a cursory glance around the dorm, then called to her friend Polly Martin who came from Onslow on the north coast.

"You coming with us," she asked her.

"Where are you going?"

When Martha explained that she wanted to take the new girls for a walk around the place Polly joined the small group.

"Yer, that's better than sitting just looking at each other," she said.

They decided to go behind the dormitory, then follow the trail along the cliffs overlooking the brown, foaming river. The path on the cliff edge was covered with loose, fine pale sand. The slopes were rough, dotted here and there with small, thick shrubs. Loose stones on the slopes made them difficult and hazardous to climb. Behind the girls was the "Big House": the superintendent's residence.

"Do you want to go down and have a closer look at the river?" Martha asked, looking at each one in turn.

"Yes," they responded with enthusiasm. As they were about to pass by the milking sheds, they heard a lot of shouting, yelling and laughter, which seemed to be coming from the flat on their left.

"Hey Martha and Polly, come down and have a game of rounders with us!" a group of girls called.

"You girls want to have a game?" asked Martha. The newcomers shook their heads. "Well, that's alright, we'll go down this way, you'll be able to get a closer look at the floods."

Polly waved to the crowd at the football oval and shouted loudly, "We're taking the girls for a walk while it's fine."

"Alright we'll see you later."

The river and the flats on either side were full to overflowing. To the girls from the East Pilbara region, this chocolate-coloured river was a new and exciting spectacle, quite different from the normal pinky coloured salt lakes, creeks and rivers back home. This sight only made Molly more aware that she was a stranger in this part of the country, as were all the others in this small group.

We are all cut off from our families, she thought and was overcome with a deep longing for the dry, rugged, red landscape of the Pilbara. Still, sighed Molly, you couldn't help being fascinated by the swirling currents and the frothy white foam that clung to the trunks of the paperbark trees and the tall river gums. As they rounded the bend of the rough road, still stepping cautiously trying to miss the muddy puddles, they were surprised to see about six or seven girls, one aged around seventeen, with a group of girls eight years old or perhaps younger, all wading across the icy cold water. The eldest girl, Edna Green, was showing the youngsters how to cross to the other side by using a long stick to measure the depth of the water. The smaller girls were following their leader, their cotton shifts were tucked into their bloomers.

"Why are they doing that?" asked Rosie, who couldn't understand why anyone would go walking in the freezing river on a cold, wet day.

"Just for something to do, that's all," Martha told her.

"When it's not raining we go for long walks all over the

place," said Polly. "But you see that big rock over there," she said, pointing across to the far side of the river. "Well, that's a woodarchies cave. Don't go over that side."

"What are these woodarchies?" asked Rosie.

"Woodarchies are little hairy men. Someone saw them for real, you know, no make up," she said seriously.

"They must be same as marbus," whispered Molly. "This is marbu country. We can't stay here, they might kill us," she added glancing at the grey limestone rock jutting out from behind the thick bushes.

She turned to her two younger sisters and was about to speak when Rosie, who was still watching the river crossing, asked Martha, "What will they do when they cross the river?"

"They will walk along the banks on the other side and when they find a safe spot Edna will decide to cross back over. And if anyone falls in they will make a big fire and stay there until all their clothes are dry then return to the compound."

"See you later," the girls said to Edna and her followers, and they continued their stroll along the muddy path up to the first paddock. Polly and Martha decided that this was as far as they were going this afternoon. They stood admiring the pleasant view from the bottom of the hill which was covered with the golden blooms of acacia shrubs and occasional bushes of bright pink flowers.

"I don't feel like climbing the hill," said Martha. "But if you do I suppose I'll have to come too."

Nobody wanted to clamber up the stony cliffs so they retraced their footsteps to where they had started.

The group were passing the spot where Edna Green's girls had made their crossing when a shrill whistle filled the air and echoed through the trees. It startled them as each one was deep in her own thoughts. They all followed the sound that came from high above them.

The whistler was leaning on the trunk of a wattle tree and

he waved to them. Polly beamed as she returned the friendly gesture. The handsome lad, who was almost eighteen, beckoned her to join him on the cliffs. She shook her head then pointed to the four girls, hoping that this would explain why she couldn't meet him.

"That's Polly's boyfriend, Jack Miller, from Mt Magnet. They gunna get married when he gets a job on a station or farm somewhere," Martha whispered as they walked ahead, leaving Polly behind to send hand signals to her beau who was now sitting on the edge of the cliff.

Polly caught up with them as they approached the cow shed. They were greeted by the cheering spectators and team mates of the winning rounders team. The crowd at the football ground had increased while they were walking along the river. Polly and Martha introduced two of the older boys to the newcomers. As they were talking they were interrupted by someone shouting loudly from a nearby building.

"Hey, who's out there?" inquired a pathetic voice from inside.

"It's me, Martha Jones and Polly Martin and four new girls."

"Can you tell my sister to bring me some meat and damper, and some tea too?" the girl asked. Her voice sounded so alone and unhappy.

"Yeah, I tell her," promised Polly. Molly, Gracie, Daisy and Rosie looked hard at the grey square building.

"What is that place?" asked Rosie, doing the talking for the other three.

"That's the 'boob', they lock anyone in there for punishment," Martha explained.

"What did that girl do?" asked Rosie.

"Who? Violet Williams? She's locked up for swearing at Miss Morgan, the teacher. She's lucky, she's only in there for two days," Martha told them about the others who had been incarcerated in the "boob".

"You should have seen the other ones who were locked up for running away," she said. "They all got seven days punishment with just bread and water. Mr Johnson shaved their heads bald and made them parade around the compound so that everyone could see them. They got the strap too."

"Oh, poor things," said Rosie.

"Everybody felt sorry for them, those three from Carnarvon," Martha said.

"Did they get far?" asked Rosie.

"No. They only got as far as Jump Up Hill, along the railway line between Gillingarra and Mogumber. They knew that the train that goes through to Geraldton slowed down there. So they waited there ready to jump into one of the goods vans. The black tracker found them there. The girls pleaded with him to let them go but he wouldn't listen, he just whipped them with his stock whip," Martha said, with anger in her voice. "He made them walk all the way back, without a break, while he rode his grey stallion like a white policeman."

"Anybody get away properly — without being caught?" enquired Rosie.

"No, lots of girls have tried to run away back to their homes but that black tracker has always caught them and brought them here again to be flogged and locked up in the 'boob'," replied Martha.

The "boob" was a place of detention once described as a small, detached concrete room with a sandy floor, with only a gleam of light and little ventilation coming through a narrow, barred opening in the north wall. Every inmate of the settlement dreaded being incarcerated in this place. Some children were forced to spend up to fourteen days in that horrible place.

Polly and Martha led the girls past the boys' dormitory, the sewing room and the front of the "Big House", down the gravelled road, through the pine plantation along the kindergarten fence to the hospital.

"That road goes down to the camps where the married couples live," said Martha, "and this one," pointing to the one on which they stood, "takes us back to the compound."

"And where does this one go?" asked Rosie, facing east and nodding in that direction.

"That's the road to Mogumber, the only one in and out of the settlement," Martha told her. "And there's a fence right around this place."

They returned to the dormitory to rest and talk. One thing on which they could all agree was that this place was certainly different from what they envisaged.

When the sons and daughters of the landed gentry and businessmen and professionals such as doctors, lawyers and politicians, were sent away to boarding schools to be educated they were likely to be given pleasant rooms that would be theirs for the duration of their schooling.

Instead of a residential school, the Aboriginal children were placed in an overcrowded dormitory. The inmates, not students, slept on cyclone beds with government-issue blankets. There were no sheets or pillow slips except on special occasions when there was an inspection by prominent officials. Then they were removed as soon as the visitors left the settlement and stored away until the next visit. On the windows there were no colourful curtains, just wire screens and iron bars. It looked more like a concentration camp than a residential school for Aboriginal children.

Back at the dormitory the girls were trying to snuggle down in their cold, uninviting beds. Molly, Daisy and Gracie began to talk normally amongst themselves, not whispering but speaking in their own relaxed manner.

"You girls can't talk blackfulla language here, you know," came the warning from the other side of the dorm. "You gotta forget it and talk English all the time."

The girls were dumbfounded, they couldn't say anything but stare at the speaker.

"That's true," said Martha in support. "I had to do the same. They tell everybody that when they come here and go to school for the first time."

Molly couldn't believe what they had just heard. "We can't talk our old wangka," she whispered. "That's awful."

"We all know it's awful," Martha told them. "But we got over that," she added calmly.

Molly lay staring at the ceiling, pondering their fate and the kind of lifestyle they could expect at this strange place and she didn't like it one bit. After a while she and the rest of the girls dozed off to sleep.

Some time later they were awakened abruptly by a loud voice telling them that the bell had gone.

"Come on, get up, tea time everybody," the voice told them.

Throughout the dormitory, sleeping forms began to rise from their narrow beds. Once again Martha took charge and led the four newcomers to the dining hall for a meal of watery stew, almost the repeat of what they had for dinner, except they also had bread and treacle. When no one was looking, Molly put all the unwanted crusts in her calico bag, and nudged her young sisters sitting either side of her to do the same.

"For later," whispered Molly.

"Well, everybody finished now?" asked Martha politely.

"Yes," said the girls softly.

"We'd better hurry, it's going to rain again." They stood briefly on the verandah to watch the thunder clouds rumbling in the west. There was a flash of lightning, followed by another.

"Quick, run," urged Martha. "It's going to pour down soon."

They reached the dormitory just in time, many of the other boys and girls were running quickly to beat the rain.

It began to fall lightly at first then as darkness approached, the wind blew strong and cold. All the inmates returned to their dormitories, the younger ones lay quietly in their beds listening to the older ones sharing with each other stories, anecdotes and hopes for the future.

After roll call and lights out, Molly listened to the slide of the bolt and the rattle of the padlock, then silence. It was at that moment this free-spirited girl knew that she and her sisters must escape from this place.

8

The Escape

*T*HE CONDITIONS WERE so degrading and inhumane in the early years of the settlement that a staff member from that period later pronounced that anyone living there, children or staff, were doomed. Perhaps a huge sign warning of the perils that lay within should have been erected at the entrance gate. However, that sign would have had no effect on the boys and girls who were abducted with government approval from their traditional homelands — because they were illiterate. But Molly, Daisy and Gracie were going to be taught to read and write, this was to be their first day at school.

It was still dark, wet and cold on that morning in August 1931 when the girls were awakened at 5.30. The little ones protested loudly and strongly at being forced to rise at that ungodly hour to leave their warm beds. Molly got up reluctantly and walked out onto the verandah, peeped through the lattice and smiled secretly to herself. Gracie and Daisy joined her but they didn't care for the grey, dismal day and said so in no uncertain terms.

The girls waited for Martha and the others to join them, then they made their way through the slushy mud near the stone wall of the staff quarters to the dining room. After a breakfast of weevily porridge, bread and tea, they returned to the dormitory to wait for the school bell.

Molly had decided the night before that she and her two sisters were not staying here. She had no desire to live in this strange place amongst people she didn't know. Anyway, she was too big to go to school, they had no right to bring her here. She was a durn-durn, a young girl who had reached puberty, she thought, touching her small budding breasts. These government people didn't know that she had been allocated a husband. But the man Burungu had passed her over for another Millungga sister and they had a four-year-old son. So, reasoned Molly, if she was old enough to be a co-wife she should be working on a station somewhere. Mr Johnson, manager of Ethel Creek Station, thought so too when he sent a telegram requesting permission to employ her and Gracie. The application was refused.

It was too early for school, so most of the smaller girls slipped back into bed. Molly, Gracie and Daisy did the same thing but they squashed into the one bed with two girls at the head and Molly at the end.

Molly finished combing her light brown hair and lay watching the movements of the others around her. At the other end of the bed Daisy and Gracie were whispering quietly to each other. Daisy, aged nine, had the same coloured hair and texture as her eldest sister, while Gracie had straight, black hair that hung down to her shoulders. It was very apparent that the three girls had inherited features from their white fathers. The only obvious Aboriginal characteristics were their dark brown eyes and their ability to control their facial expressions, so that when they reached maturity they would develop the look of a quiet, dignified Aboriginal woman from the Pilbara region.

The other girls were now getting ready for school, and the three watched quietly amidst all the activity. Bossing and bullying was everywhere around them and there were cries and squeals of, "Don't, you're hurting my head," as the tangled knots were combed out with tiny, fragile combs.

"Oh, Mummy, Daddy, Mummy, Daddy, my head," yelled a young girl, who stamped her feet and tried to pull away from her torturer, an older, well-built girl who seemed to have adopted the girl as her baby sister. They performed this ritual together every morning before school.

"Come on, you girls," ordered Martha Jones as she passed by their bed. "The school bell's gone. Don't be late on your first day."

"Alright, we're coming as soon as we empty the toilet bucket," answered Molly softly.

"I'll wait for you then," said Martha.

"No, don't wait we'll follow you, we know where the school is."

"Alright then, we'll go along. Come on, Rosie," she said as she rushed out of the door into the cold, drizzily morning.

As soon as the other girls left the dormitory, Molly beckoned her two sisters to come closer to her, then she whispered urgently, "We're not going to school, so grab your bags. We're not staying here." Daisy and Gracie were stunned and stood staring at her.

"What did you say?" asked Gracie.

"I said, we're not staying here at the settlement, because we're going home to Jigalong."

Gracie and Daisy weren't sure whether they were hearing correctly or not.

"Move quickly," Molly ordered her sisters. She wanted to be miles away before their absence was discovered. Time was of the essence.

Her two young sisters faced each other, both looking very scared and confused. Daisy turned to Molly and said nervously, "We're frightened, Dgudu. How are we going to find our way back home to Jigalong? It's a long way from home."

Molly leaned against the wall and said confidently, "I

know it's a long way to go but it's easy. We'll find the rabbit-proof fence and follow that all the way home."

"We gunna walk all the way?" asked Daisy.

"Yeah," replied Molly, getting really impatient now. "So don't waste time."

The task of finding the rabbit-proof fence seemed like a simple solution for a teenager whose father was an inspector who travelled up and down the fences, and whose grandfather had worked with him. Thomas Craig told her often enough that the fence stretched from coast to coast, south to north across the country. It was just a matter of locating a stretch of it then following it to Jigalong. The two youngsters trusted their big sister because she was not only the eldest but she had always been the bossy one who made all the decisions at home. So they did the normal thing and said, "Alright, Dgudu, we'll run away with you."

They snatched up their meagre possessions and put them into calico bags and pulled the long drawstrings and slung them around their necks. Each one put on two dresses, two pairs of calico bloomers and a coat.

Gracie and Daisy were about to leave when Molly told them to, "Wait. Take those coats off. Leave them here."

"Why?" asked Gracie.

"Because they're too heavy to carry."

The three sisters checked to make sure they hadn't missed anything then, when they were absolutely satisfied, Molly grabbed the galvanised bucket and ordered Gracie to get hold of the other side and walk quickly trying not to spill the contents as they made their way to the lavatories. Daisy waited under the large pine tree near the stables. She reached up and broke a small twig that was hanging down low and was examining it closely when the other two joined her.

"Look, Dgudu, like grass indi?" asked Daisy, passing the twig to Molly to feel.

"Youay," she said, as she gave it to Gracie who crushed

the green pine needles into her small hands and sniffed them. She liked the smell and was about to give her opinion when Molly reminded them that they didn't have time to stand around examining pine needles.

"Come on, run, you two," she said sharply as she started to run towards the river.

Many young people had stood under the same big pine tree and waited while someone went into the stable or the garage to distract Maitland, the caretaker and stableman. Then they would give the signal that the coast was clear and everyone would dash into the grainary and fill their empty fruit tins with wheat from one of the opened bags at the back of the shed. Some of it was roasted on flat tins over the hot coals, the rest was saved to fill initials that had been dug into the sloping embankment of firm yellow sand along the cliffs. These were left until the first rain came, then all the inmates would rush down to inspect the cliffs. This grass graffiti revealed the new summer romances between the older boys and girls. But these three girls from the East Pilbara had no intention of participating, they had a more important task ahead of them.

On they went, dashing down the sandy slope of the cliffs, dodging the small shrubs on the way and following the narrow path to the flooded river. They slowed down only when they reached the bottom. Molly paused briefly, glancing at the pumping shed on their right where they had been the day before. Turning towards it she said to Gracie and Daisy, "This way." She ran for about 25 metres, crashing into the thick paperbark trees and the branches of the river gums that blocked their path.

Molly strode on as best as she could along the muddy banks, pausing only to urge her young sisters to hurry up and try to keep up with her. She kept up that pace until she saw what she thought to be a likely spot to cross the swift flowing river.

The three girls watched the swirling currents and the

white and brown frothy foam that clung to the trunks of the young river gums and clumps of tea-trees. They didn't know that this became one of the most popular spots during the hot summer days. This was the local swimming pool that would be filled with naked or semi-naked brown bodies, laughing, splashing, swimming and diving into the cool brown water during the long summer afternoons. Every now and then, the swimmers would sit on the coarse river sand and yank ugly, brown, slimey leeches off their bodies and impale them on sticks and turn them inside out and plunge them into the hot burning mud. The next day the swimmers would pull the sticks out of the sand and gloat at the shrivelled dry skins that once were horrible little creatures, ready to suck all the blood from their bodies — or so the young people were led to believe.

"The river is too deep and fast here, let's try up further," Molly said, leading the way through the thick young suckers and washed-up logs. They continued along the bank making slow progress through the obstacles that nature had left in their path. At last they came to a section in the river that seemed narrow enough to cross.

"We'll try here," said Molly as she bent down to pick up a long stick. She slid down the bank into the river and began measuring its depth just as she had seen Edna Green do the previous afternoon, while Daisy and Gracie watched patiently on the bank.

"Nah, too deep," Molly said in disgust. "Not here."

"Gulu, Dgudu," cried the youngsters as they ran to follow her through the wet foliage.

The three girls walked along the muddy banks for another 25 metres when they came to a clearing, devoid of any shrubs or young suckers, where the floods had receded.

In a couple of weeks' time, this place would become a muddy skating rink where the girls of the settlement would spend hours having fun skating up and down the slippery mud. The idea was to skate by placing one foot in front of the other and maintain your balance for a couple of metres at least. The boys had their own skating area further up in a more secluded place amongst the thick tea-tree shrub. Peeping toms never existed in those days, each group respected each other's privacy. Nearby, a huge fire would be lit and kept stoked. When everyone had finished skating in the slippery mud they would dive into the icy cold river to wash off the mud, then dry themselves by the roaring fire, dress, and return to the compound.

Molly decided to follow the paths made by the cattle. Another attempt was made to cross the river but once again proved unsuccessful. She walked on angrily, pushing the thick growth of eucalyptus suckers roughly aside, at the same time urging Daisy and Gracie to walk faster. But they decided that it was much safer at a distance and they followed her muddy footprints in silence without any questions, trusting her leadership totally.

They were still fighting their way through the tea-trees for almost an hour when they heard Molly call out to them somewhere down the track. "Yardini! Bukala! Bukala!"

Daisy and Gracie ran as fast as they could along the muddy path until they reached her. Molly was standing near a large river gum. As they stood gasping for wind she said, "We gunna cross here."

As three pairs of eager eyes examined it closely, they knew that they had found the perfect place to cross the flooded river. A tree leaned over the water creating a natural bridge for them to cross safely to the other side.

The girls scraped mud from their feet then climbed onto the trunk and walked cautiously to the end then swung down off the limb onto the slippery, muddy bank on the other side. They sloshed through the wet, chocolate-coloured banks for at least another two hours, then decided to rest amongst the thick reeds behind the tall river gums.

A few minutes later, Molly stood up and told her young sisters to get up. "We go kyalie now all the way." They obeyed without any protests. Ducking under the hanging branches of the paperbark trees they hurried as best they could, stomping on the reeds and bull rushes that covered the banks of the fast flowing river. The only sounds that could be heard were the startled birds fluttering above as they left their nests in fright, and the *slish, slosh* of the girls' feet as they trampled over the bull rushes.

Now the question is, how does anyone keep travelling in a northerly direction on a dismal, grey day without a map or compass? It would be difficult for an adult without the most thorough knowledge of bushcraft not to become disoriented and lost in a strange part of the country where the landscape is filled with thick undergrowth and without the sun to guide the way. Well, Molly, this fourteen-year-old girl, had no fear because the wilderness was her kin. It always provided shelter, food and sustenance. She had learned and developed bushcraft skills and survival techniques from an expert, her step-father, a former nomad from the desert. She memorised the direction in which they had travelled: it was north by car from Perth to Mogumber siding, then west to the settlement. Also, she had caught a glimpse of the sun when it appeared from behind the rain clouds at various intervals during their tour of the place on their first day. That enabled her to determine that she was moving in the right direction.

The girls were relieved to leave the sloshy, muddy banks that were covered with reeds. Further up from the river bank grew stands of flooded gum. These were tall trees with straight, white trunks and a dense canopy of leafy branches. Amongst them grew the tightly bunched swamp paperbarks that were so difficult for the three girls to forge a path through.

Once they had left the flooded river area the three were able to speed up their progress as they stomped over the wet grass on the flats and passed through an open landscape and under giant marri gums with thick trunks covered with grey to brownish-grey flaky bark.

The girls trod gingerly over dry and decayed honky nuts that had fallen from the marri gum, trying not to slip. Nearby, grasslands led into a fenced-off area of sandy slopes filled with marri gums, banksia and prickly bark or coastal blackbutt. The sand plains that the girls came to over the rise were covered with acacia thickets and prickly grevilleas that scratched their bare legs. They tried not to let the discomfort bother them but this was difficult in the cold weather. Stepping around the prickly, dense undergrowth and over the ground cover onto patches of white sand, the girls continued on at their steady pace, pausing only to climb through boundary fences.

Molly was pleased that the mud and slush and the swamp paperbarks were behind them. They were now on the heathlands. The heathlands of Western Australia contain some of this country's most beautiful and unusual wildflowers. The girls stood among the banksia trees admiring the magnificent flowers of the many species that thrive in the sandy plains. They knelt to have a closer look and to touch the beautiful kangaroo paw flowers, from the smallest — the yellow and orange cat's paw — to the yellow and the green and black varieties. The most famous variety is the red and green kangaroo paw, our state emblem.

There are so many colourful and magnificent flowers in this part of our state and because they bloom throughout the year, there is always some plant displaying its beauty in these heathlands.

It started to sprinkle again; the girls looked up to the sky and saw that there were only scattered clouds, so they trudged on unperturbed through the open forest of banksia, prickly bark and Christmas trees, that covered the low sand dunes. Eventually, the showers passed over them heading inland and the girls tramped through the thick wet grass.

Molly, Daisy and Gracie tried not to look at the dark blue hills in the distance on their right. They were content to keep walking north at an easy pace that suited them well. Their sights were fixed on what lay before them.

They had covered a lot of ground since crossing the main branch of the Moore River, over hills and sand dunes, and across the white sand plains. Yes, they were making very good progress through the open banksia forests and they had covered a wide area of coastal, sandy heaths and had the pleasure to see a variety of flowers.

The girls were fascinated by the bright orange and white and the red and yellow conical shaped banksia flowers. They pulled the branches down so that they could examine them more closely. Beneath the banksia trees, the ground was covered with a tangled undergrowth of plants, creepers, tufts of grass, decaying leaves and dry banksia nuts. It was almost impossible to find a patch of clean, white sand amongst all that for the girls to pass through without scratching or stinging their legs on the prickly acacia bushes. Although, it wasn't too bad when it was raining because the cool drops washed and soothed the scratches on their skins.

They were almost past the clumps of banksia trees when they heard heavy foot falls. It sounded like someone or something was heading their way. At that moment it began to sprinkle but they could still hear those footsteps. They were coming closer. There was another flash of lightning and in the distance they heard a rumble of thunder. The footsteps were even closer.

"Quick," whispered Molly and all three dived head first into the thicket and slid on their stomachs as flat and low as they could, not daring to breathe. They kept very still, frozen with fear as they lay under the cover of the tangled scrub and waited for whatever it was to appear. Molly had no intention of being caught only to be sent back to the settlement to be punished by the authorities.

The footsteps were so close now that the ground was vibrating and they could feel every step it took. Then they saw it. The frightened girls couldn't believe their eyes, and they couldn't move if they wanted to. They could only lie there staring at the "thing" that was emerging from behind the banksia trees.

Gracie started to say something in a low whisper but the words came out as an inaudible stutter. She tried once more, but the result was the same, so she gave up and shut her eyes tightly and began to swallow deeply, trying desperately to control her fear. For several minutes after the "thing" had gone by, its footsteps still thundering along, the girls remained on the prickly leaves, pondering whether or not it was safe to move. Their young hearts were thumping right up into their ears. They lay shivering with fear.

It was another few seconds before they regained their composure and their fear subsided. Only then could they rise and stand firmly on their feet without shaking, to continue their trek homewards.

"That was a marbu, indi Dgudu?" said Daisy, still obviously shaken by what she had seen.

"Youay, it was a marbu alright," Molly agreed. "A proper marbu," she added shivering as she remembered the frightening image.

Yes, the thing fitted the description of a marbu, a sharp-toothed, flesh-eating evil spirit that has been around since the Dreamtime. The old people always told children to be careful and to watch out for them and now the three girls had finally seen one.

"That marbu had a funny head and long hair. He was a big one alright," said Daisy.

There seems to be only one logical explanation to that phenomenon, and that was the so-called marbu may have been a particularly large, hairy Aboriginal man with prominent facial features who was running to beat the storm that was brewing and the fast approaching nightfall. The man's giant-like stature may have played upon the girls' imaginations and their belief in a mythical being of the Dreamtime stories. But to these children from the Western Desert it was genuine and no one could tell them otherwise.

"Quickly," urged Molly. "Let us get away from this place." The sight of the marbu had unnerved her so she was also very scared.

"There might be others around here. We gotta get away from this bad place," she added urgently with a slight tremble in her voice. "It's getting dark. We have to find a good, safe place to make a camp for the night."

Molly scanned the surrounding countryside swiftly, then paused and pointed to a small range of sand dunes not far from the forest of banksia trees.

The two younger sisters nodded. They could see the shallow valley of deep sand and the sand dunes on the left and began making their way towards them.

"See that," said Molly when they reached the sand dunes, pointing to the rabbit warrens. "We'll just dig one. We have to make it big enough for three of us to fit into."

"We gunna sleep in the bunna like rabbits too, Dgudu?" asked Grace.

"Youay, nobody gunna look in a rabbit burrow for us, indi," replied Molly confidently.

"That's true, no one will find us in there," said Daisy as she joined them.

So, crouching on their knees, they dug furiously with their elbows almost touching each other's. Very soon they managed to widen and deepen a deserted burrow to make a slightly cramped but warm, dry shelter. This was their first night out in the bush since leaving their homes in the East Pilbara.

Before the three sisters settled down to sleep they ate some of the dry crusts of bread and drank the cool, clear water from the pools at the bottom of the valley. They had nibbled on some of the bread while they walked during the afternoon.

Molly had chosen a rabbit burrow that faced east because she had noticed that the rain came from the west over the coast. They would be well protected from the wet and cold while they slept.

Crawling in one at a time, they cuddled up together in the rabbit burrow, wriggling and twisting around until they were comfortable. Soon, with the warmth of their young bodies and weariness, Daisy and Gracie drifted off to sleep. With their heads resting on their calico bags at the entrance and their feet touching the sandy wall at the back of the burrow they felt safe and warm.

While her two sisters were sleeping, Molly lay quietly listening to the rain falling steadily on the sand outside. She was too tense and had too much on her mind to relax and go to sleep just yet. But despite that she felt safe inside the rabbit burrow. Tomorrow, she told herself, I will find the rabbit-proof fence and it will take us all the way home to Jigalong. The thought raised her hopes and a few minutes later she too drifted off into sleep.

Suddenly Molly and Daisy were awakened by the frightened cries of Gracie, "Dgudu, Dgudu, where are you?"

"I am here, right next to you. What's wrong?" Molly asked.

"Dgudu, that marbu, he came back and pulled me by the hair. He tried to drag me outside," she said shivering and sobbing loudly.

"Shush, don't cry," said Molly as she put her arm around her. "It was just a bad dream. Go back to sleep. I won't let anything bad happen to you," she promised.

Molly managed to calm Gracie and soon they all fell asleep once again.

The next morning, very early, the three girls were awakened by the thump, thumping of rabbits from adjoining burrows.

"It's not worth trying to catch any rabbits this time," said Molly disappointedly.

"Why can't we catch any rabbits, Dgudu?" queried Gracie, brushing the pale yellow sand off her legs, while trying rather feebly not to think of the aroma and taste of a freshly cooked rabbit.

At that moment Gracie spied one and gave chase, caught and killed it.

"What did you do that for?" asked Molly angrily, "I told you, we got no matches to make a fire to cook it."

Gracie replied, "Well, I'm hungry," as she searched around for a sharp object with which she could gut the rabbit. Finding none, she swore loudly then threw it hard on the ground, and stomped off over the thick prickly undergrowth. So instead of rabbit roasted over the coals for breakfast, there was plenty of fresh water from the pools at the bottom of the valley and stale crusts from the settlement. This was their second meal on the run.

"Dgudu," said Gracie, "we should go back to the settlement. We might die. Come on, we go back," she pleaded. She was still shaken by the sight of a real marbu. There might be more lurking in the woodlands.

"You want to go back to the settlement," retorted Molly angrily. "You heard what they'll do to us. They'll shave our heads bald and give us a big hiding and lock us up in the little gaol," she said shaking her finger, while Daisy stood by silently watching and listening.

"You want to go back, you're mad. We three came down together, and we will go home together. We're not going to die in the bush," she assured her. "So let's move," she added finally as she strode off into the acacia thickets.

Gracie became stubborn and refused to move. "I'm hungry Dgudu. I want some mundu not just bread and water."

Molly stopped and turned to face her young sister.

"I know that. We are all hungry for meat," she reminded

her. But most of all they were missing their mothers and wished that they were back home with them.

Molly walked back to the dejected younger sister and put her arm around her shoulder and told her gently, "Don't worry, we will find something to eat, you'll see. This country's different from ours, so we gotta learn to find their bush tucker, that's all. Come on, let's go along now."

Molly managed to coax Gracie out of her stubbornness and they walked briskly to where Daisy sat playing with some dry banksia nuts. She stood up when she saw them coming and the three of them walked northwards.

The weather remained unchanged. The skies were grey and a cold wind was blowing across the bushland. It looked like more rain was coming their way. Gracie and Daisy missed their warm gaberdine coats and they longed for a meal of meat, hot damper and sweet tea. They continued north, through the wet countryside, never knowing what was waiting for them over the next hill.

The three were pacing in good style, covering the miles in an easy manner. Soon they found that they were entering a landscape dominated by clumps of grass trees. Interspersed amongst them were zamia palms and scattered here and there were a few marri, wandoo and mallee gums. The girls descended a hill into a stand of tall flooded river gums and paperbarks and reached the edge of a river and stared at the flowing water. They had come to a branch of the Moore River.

"How are we going to get across the river, Dgudu?" asked Daisy.

"I don't know yet," she replied as she began to search along the banks until she found a suitable place to cross.

"Up here," she called out to her sisters. "We will cross over on this fence. Come on," encouraged Molly as she tucked her dress into the waist of her bloomers. With her calico bag slung around her neck, she clung to the top strand of fence wire, while her feet were planted firmly on the bottom strand.

"See, it's strong enough to hold us," she assured them. "Watch me and follow, come on."

Slowly and gingerly they stepped onto the fence wire, not daring to look down at the brown flooded river below. The water swirled and splashed against their feet. They tried to shut out the sounds and sights of the gushing water and instead they concentrated on reaching the muddy bank on the other side. They were worried about their precious bags that contained all their worldly goods, which wasn't much at all, just an extra pair of bloomers, a frock and their small mirrors, combs and a cake of Lifeboy soap. However, they made it safely.

On their second day they came into a section of bushland that had been ravished by fire. All the trees and the grass under them was burnt black. In a few weeks' time, however, this charcoal landscape would be revived by the rain. It would come alive and be a green wilderness again, full of beautiful flowers and animals that are wonderfully and uniquely Australian. The three girls walked in silence over the next hill where they saw a most unexpected but very welcome sight indeed. Coming towards them were two Mardu men on their way home from a hunting trip. Gracie and Daisy were so pleased to see them that they almost ran to meet them, but Molly held the girls back and whispered softly, "Wait."

So the three girls waited for the men to come closer. When they saw the men's catch, they drooled — a cooked kangaroo and two murrandus. The girls were more interested in the bush tucker than in the two hunters who introduced themselves and told the girls that they were from Marble Bar.

"Where are you girls going?" asked one of the men.

"We are running away back home to Jigalong," replied Molly.

"Well, you girls want to be careful, this country different from ours, you know," advised the old man with white hair and a bushy white beard.

"They got a Mardu policeman, a proper cheeky fullah. He flog 'em young gel runaway gels like you three," he added very concerned for them as they were from the Pilbara too.

"Youay," said Molly. "We heard about him at the settlement."

"He follow runaway gels and take 'em back to the settlement. He's a good tracker, that Mardu," the old man told them.

"We know that, the girl from Port Hedland already told us about him," replied Molly who was very confident that the black tracker would not be able to follow their path because all their footprints would have been washed away by the rain.

The men gave them a kangaroo tail and one of the goannas. They shook hands with the girls and turned to walk away when the younger man remembered something.

"Here, you will need these," he said as he held up a box of matches. Then he emptied another box and filled it with salt.

The girls thanked them and said goodbye.

"Don't forget now, go quickly. That Kimberley bloke will be looking for you right now, this time now."

It was highly unlikely that an attempt to track them down in this weather would even be considered but Molly wasn't taking any chances. They would only stop when she was satisfied that it was safe to rest.

The miles they had covered should have been adequate according to Daisy and Gracie but no, their elder sister made them trudge along until dusk. Then the three young girls set about preparing a wuungku made from branches of trees and shrubs. They searched under the thick bushes and gathered up handfuls of dry twigs and enough leaves to start a small fire. There was no shortage of trees and bushes around their shelter as they grew in abundance; quite different from the sparse landscape of the Western Desert. Each girl carried armfuls of wood and dropped them on the ground near the fire to dry as they had decided that it was safe enough to keep the fire burning all night. They made the fire in a hole in the ground in the centre of the shelter.

After a supper of kangaroo tail, goanna and the last crust of bread, washed down with rain water, they loaded more wood on the fire and slept warm and snug in the rough bush shelter around the fire.

The next morning, the girls were awakened by the sounds of birds fluttering and chirping all around them. The rain had stopped but the wind was blowing strong and cold. The clouds were scattered about like huge balls of cotton wool and the sun was trying hard to shine through the gaps. It may have been wishful thinking on their part but the weather looked promising.

For breakfast they ate what was left over from supper with a refreshing drink of water. When they had finished they quickly removed the firewood that was still burning and covered it with wet sand and moved on. Molly looked up at the sky and said confidently, "More rain coming," pointing to the west where the white, fluffy clouds were now being pushed aside by grey rain clouds.

"Never mind," she said. "It's good because that Mardu policeman can't follow us now. We lose all our tracks anyhow. The rain will wash them all away." She and her sisters were safe from capture for the time being.

"Come on, walk faster, the rain is a long way off yet," she told them, hoping her estimation was accurate, because she wanted to be a long way away by nightfall. In this weather and in this sand plain country the girls had been covering 24 to 30 kilometres a day. They each realised that they must push on further into the wilderness, steadily covering as much ground as they could during the daylight hours. By midday, the girls were hit with pangs of hunger. Gracie was feeling very irritable and began to stamp her feet in protest and dawdled along. Suddenly she got caught in the dense, tangled scarlet runner creepers, she overbalanced and fell onto the wet ground with a thud. She lay there moaning and groaning softly to herself.

"We gunna die. We got nothing to eat."

"Oh shut up and stop whinging," ordered Molly as she helped her up on her feet. "We gotta hurry up."

Molly was losing patience with her younger sister. At that moment the most important thing on her mind was distance; the more land they covered in this weather, the less chance they had of being captured. Getting lost or walking around in circles may have signalled the end of their escape but Molly kept reminding them to be brave and to conquer their fears. There was little danger in this part of the country, as there were no poisonous snakes lurking about at this time of year.

Gracie withdrew into herself, refusing to talk. She just followed Molly and Daisy in a trance, eyes straight ahead, looking neither right or left, silent and sullen. Suddenly Molly shouted excitedly, "Look over there." Shaken out of her grey mood, Gracie was interested in what her big sister had seen.

"What is it, Dgudu?" Daisy wanted to know.

Daisy and Gracie looked up to see the rabbit burrows in the sand dunes.

"We're not sleeping in the bunna again, eh Dgudu?" asked Gracie.

"No," replied Molly. "We gunna catch them to eat."

The girls hadn't eaten since the morning and it was now very late in the afternoon. Stumbling on another rabbit warren was indeed an exciting find. They were starving, and the prospect of a feed of meat spurred them on.

"We will block all the burrows except that one in the

middle, alright?" suggested Molly. So the three set about blocking all the entrances, leaving only one open. Then they sat down quietly behind some acacia bushes and waited.

After what seemed like ages, out came the rabbits. First one, then two, four, then more.

"Now," ordered Molly. "Go." She leaped up and chased the rabbits and the others joined in. Molly and Gracie were excellent runners, they caught a rabbit each, while their knock-kneed youngest sister missed them. She could not catch even the slowest in the group.

It was past dusk when they found a suitable place to make a shelter and camp for the night. The girls were in good spirits as they made a huge fire in a hole in the ground and cooked the rabbits in the ashes, after gutting them roughly by using a sharp point of a green stick. They ate one of them for supper that evening with water from a soak they found in the limestone rocks near the camp site. The other rabbit was saved for breakfast.

Molly rose early the next morning to stoke up the dying fire, the other two were content to lie there in their cosy shelter for a couple of hours more, they got an hour at least. Molly sat warming herself by the fire, listening to the sounds of the heathlands.

There were lots of black and white Willie wagtails and other beautiful birds darting in and out of the trees and shrubs but she still missed the sounds of the finches and white cockatoos of her home.

Thoughts of home reminded her of the distance they had to cover and as quickly as possible.

"Come on, get up," ordered Molly. "We can't stay here all day. We got a long way to go yet," she added impatiently as she broke the rabbit in three portions.

There was no response so she called again for them to get up.

"Move, come on," she urged.

"Oh, alright, we're coming," said Daisy as she shook the sleeping Gracie.

When her sisters joined her for breakfast, Molly said, "Don't eat it all, save some for later."

They nodded in agreement as they bit into the tough flesh of the cold cooked rabbit. Once breakfast was over, they drank the soak water and washed their hands and faces, drying them with the calico bags, then they continued onwards, over the sand hills and through the banksia woodlands, with their acacia thickets and thick clumps of heath. Scattered among them were tall marri gums and mallee. The drier conditions along the coastal sand plains made bushes grow thick and small, and the trees were stunted because of the sandy soil.

Molly was pleased that there was no shortage of trees and shrubs to hide under. They grew in abundance, quite different from the sparse landscape of the north-west.

The morning was pleasant, everything was quiet and peaceful. The sun was shining through the clouds and the raindrops on the leaves and spiders' webs sparkled like diamonds. Below them was an open grassland of lush green pastures that would soon become a field of bright yellow dandelions. By their manner one could have thought that the girls were taking a leisurely stroll in the bush. They appeared very relaxed as they walked along together. Then all of a sudden they stopped and gasped, all three of them looked then dropped behind the shrubs and peeped around cautiously to watch from this safe distance.

In the clearing in the far end of the paddock were two of the biggest and blackest kangaroos they had ever seen.

"Look at them, they're standing up and fighting like men," whispered Molly. "But they can't see us up here."

"I'm frightened, Dgudu," Gracie whispered.

"Me too, Dgudu," said Daisy moving closer to her older sister.

The sight of these big boomers had unnerved the

younger sisters and Molly wasn't feeling brave herself. The fear of venturing into unknown territory had resurfaced and she didn't want that to happen.

"Come on, let's get away from here. We'll walk around them. They won't see us if we crawl behind these bushes," Molly whispered. "And keep your eyes on them all the way to the end of the paddock."

"Ready, come on," she ordered. Molly began to crawl on her hands and knees with great discomfort as the ground was covered with prickles and dry twigs and leaves. She tried to make a clear path for her two sisters to follow.

The two smaller girls felt threatened by the size of the big boomers so they were glad to be out of sight. They didn't want to be attacked by kangaroos, and they were very relieved when they had climbed the boundary fence. It was only then that they could feel safe again. The three girls sat on a fallen log, trying to recover from the shocking sight of the fighting animals.

"Those boomers are bigger than the ones we got at home, indi Dgudu," said Gracie fearfully, "and cheeky fullahs too."

Daisy and Molly both answered together. "Youay."

The trio sat quietly on the dead log. The silence was broken suddenly by an alarmed Molly, who pulled Gracie up roughly by the arms.

"Run under that big tree over there," she yelled, pointing to a large banksia tree. "Climb up and hide there. You too Daisy. Come on."

When she saw that they had difficulty getting up, she ran over to help them. She pushed her two young sisters up into the branches and told them not to move unless she said so.

Although the two youngsters could not see any danger they obeyed without question, they trusted her with their lives. After all, hadn't their big sister proved herself to be a worthy leader. Her self-control and courage had never faltered throughout the trek.

So there they lay, stretched out on the rough branches not daring to move, just silently waiting and listening. At last they heard it. It was a plane, a search plane sent out to look for them, these runaway girls. Sitting very still, the girls listened while the plane circled above them, then it gave up and returned home. Several minutes passed before Molly decided it was safe to climb down from their hiding places in the trees. Once they were on the ground they quickened their pace, keeping close to the trees in case they needed to hide again. They walked in silence, concentrating on movement, distance and safety. No one took any notice of the change in the weather until they were caught in the showers. It was only then that they realised that the sun and blue sky had disappeared. There was nothing but dark rain clouds. It seemed hopeless to try to find shelter; they were drenched and their hair hung limp and dripping with water. Just when they were overcome with gloom and despair, they heard the most welcomed sounds with which they were each familiar. At that moment they realised just how much they had missed them and they were overcome with depression.

It was noon and these were the sounds of fowls, squeaky windmills and barking dogs, that reminded them of Jigalong, Walgun and Murra Munda stations, but most of all these sounds brought back memories of their loved ones who remained there. Pangs of hunger overcame their nostalgia. As they approached the farmhouse Molly gently urged the two sisters forward.

"Go in there and ask the missus for some food to eat. Hurry up. I'll wait here," she said as she settled down behind the thick trunk of a marri gum.

Daisy and Gracie went willingly because they were feeling very hungry and here was the chance to find something more substantial than what they had been forced to live on so far. The last remaining pieces of rabbit leftover from breakfast had all gone.

Approaching the farmhouse slowly, they looked about them. Glancing at the barking dogs they saw that both were chained near their kennels but they still gave the girls a scare as they tried to rush past them. Fortunately the strong chains held. The girls opened the wooden gate and were greeted by a little four-year-old girl who was playing with her toys on the large verandah.

"Come inside," she said warmly as she opened the door. "My name is Susan," she added as she rushed inside.

"Mummy," she yelled, "there's two girls outside and they're all wet."

Daisy and Gracie didn't accept the child's invitation to go inside, but stood politely on the verandah, letting the water trickle to the hems of their dresses then onto the timbered verandah.

Little Susan's mother came to the door and asked them, "Are you the runaways from the settlement?"

"Yes," they replied shyly.

"Where's the other one?" she asked.

"She's outside near the big tree, on the other side of the fence," Gracie informed her.

"Go and tell her to come inside and dry herself while I make something to eat," the woman said.

When she saw their reluctance, she smiled and said, "It's alright, you won't be reported." So Gracie dashed out in the rain to bring Molly inside the warm kitchen.

The woman, whose name was Mrs Flanagan, had received a phone call from Superintendent Neal on Tuesday afternoon asking her to watch out for three absconders and to report to him if she saw them. Mrs Flanagan asked the girls a lot of questions, especially about their ultimate destination.

"We are going to find the rabbit-proof fence and follow it all the way home to Jigalong," Molly said.

"Well, I'm afraid you're going the wrong way. The rabbit-proof fence is not north. You must go east towards Ayres

Find and Wubin. If you keep going north you will come to the coastal towns of either Dongara or Geraldton."

Mrs Flanagan made thick mutton and tomato chutney sandwiches, which the three girls stared at as if mesmerised. The aroma was overpowering, they could almost taste the cold mutton and crusty bread. Then they devoured them greedily, like the starving youngsters they were. These were followed by generous pieces of fruit cake and a cup of sweet, milky tea. A feeling of contentment prevailed in the comfortable, warm, dry farmhouse kitchen. Soon they became quite drowsy.

The girls watched as Mrs Flanagan filled a couple of brown paper bags with tea leaves, sugar, flour and salt and half a leg of mutton and a chunk of fruit cake and bread. She took three large empty fruit tins and said, "You will need these to boil your tea in. It may be easier to carry them in your bags. Have you all had enough to eat?"

"Yes, thank you," they said. They almost added, "missus" but managed to stop quickly.

"Right then, come with me and I'll give you some dry clothes to change into, and warm coats," she said as she led the way outside to a large shed opposite the house where there was a small storeroom. Inside was stored farm machinery, implements and grain. Mrs Flanagan pulled out some old army uniforms — a greatcoat for Molly and jackets for Gracie and Daisy.

"Here, you'd better take these too," she said, handing them some wheat bags. "Use them as capes to protect you from the rain and cold winds."

Mrs Flanagan demonstrated how to make a cape by pushing one corner into the other. With their army coats and bag capes they were warm and dry.

Watching the three girls disappear into the open woodlands, she said loudly to herself, "Those girls are too young to be wandering around in the bush. They'll perish for sure. They don't know this part of the country. And the three of them with just dresses on. It's a wonder they didn't catch colds or worse, pneumonia. I'll have to report this to Mr Neal for their own good before they get lost and die in the bush," she said. "It's my duty."

When she had made her decision she went inside and lifted the earpiece of the telephone, turned the handle and listened, then she spoke into the mouthpiece.

"Good afternoon, Christine," she greeted the girl at the exchange. "Has Kath Watson had her baby yet?"

"No, not yet," the girl replied. "It's due any day now."

After a few minutes, Mrs Flanagan had learned all the news of the local townspeople.

"Christine," she said, "can you send a telegram to Mr Neal, the Superintendent of the Moore River Native Settlement, please."

"Yes. Just hold the line for one moment."

Mrs Flanagan made a fresh pot of tea, satisfied that she had done the right thing. Anyway, she told herself, those three girls from the north-west would fare no better than the other runaways. Once they reached the railway line they would decide to sit and wait for the train, then they would be handed over to the police at the next railway siding or station. They always get caught.

A kilometre away, the three sisters agreed that from that point onwards they would follow a routine. Whenever they arrived at a farmhouse or station homestead, Daisy and Gracie would enter the yard and ask for food while Molly waited a safe distance away, out of sight, where she could watch them. Thankfully, food was never refused. These handouts sustained the girls during their long trek home.

Molly decided to continue in the same direction for a couple of hours at least — just to foil their would-be captors whom the lady at the farmhouse may have contacted.

"We go that way," she said, pointing north-east. "Not kukarda. That midgerji know which way we're going now."

"You know, we shouldn't have told her where we were

heading," Molly said regrettably. "They might have someone waiting for us along the rabbit-proof fence. Never mind. We'll go this way for now."

So they walked quickly, wearing their wheat bag capes and military coats that protected them from the rain.

They had enough food for a day or two, so if they quickened their pace they would reach somewhere safe before dark and make a warm, dry shelter for the night.

The girls were still in the coastal heathlands among scattered tall shrubs and low trees, having passed through the tall trees and open grasslands of the marri woodlands. Molly, Daisy and Gracie had grown used to the landscape of the coastal plains. They liked the Geraldton wax flowers and the dainty, white tea-tree flowers.

This drier, more northerly section of the heathlands, with its pure white and grey sandy soils, put the girls at a disadvantage. There were no tall trees with dense foliage under which they could hide from search parties.

Darkness and the drizzling rain forced them to find a spot to make camp for the night.

"Here!" said Molly as she broke off a thick heath bush. "This is a good place to make our camp. Come on, hurry up and break more bushes."

In a few minutes they had erected a cosy, firm little shelter under the bushes, then they rushed around and collected dry twigs and leaves to make a fire.

This warmed them while they enjoyed their supper of cold mutton, bread, fruit cake and sweet, black tea. The fire and food made them feel more relaxed and helped them to talk and laugh together — a ritual that had been sadly missing during the past few days. Soon the heat made them drowsy, so they settled into their shelter and in no time at all, they were fast asleep.

The next morning the skies were clear. There was no rain, only raindrops drip, dripping from the leaves of the trees and shrubs onto the sand and dead leaves beneath.

Patches of grass were still wet and were dropping heavily with water. Just looking out made the girls shiver. None of them wanted to leave their cosy shelter. Gracie and Daisy waited until their big sister got up and made a fire, then crawled out to join her.

"There's enough water in my fruit tin to make tea," Molly said.

Gracie watched her older sister break the meat, bread and cake as fairly as she could with her hands. They had no knife to cut the food evenly and to stir the sugar in their tea they simply broke a strong eucalyptus twig.

While the three runaways were having a quiet breakfast in the bush, news of their escape was spreading across the country. Mrs Flanagan was not the only person who knew or guessed their whereabouts, the whole state was told about them when this item appeared in the *West Australian* on 11 August 1931:

MISSING NATIVE GIRLS

The Chief Protector of Aborigines, Mr A.O. Neville, is concerned about three native girls, ranging from eight to 15 years of age, who a week ago, ran away from the Moore River Native Settlement, Mogumber. They came in from the Nullagine district recently, Mr O'Neville said yesterday, and, being very timid, were scared by their new quarters, apparently, and fled in the hope of getting back home. Some people saw them passing New Norcia, when they seemed to be heading northeast. The children would probably keep away from habitations and he would be grateful if any person who saw them would notify him promptly. "We have been searching high and low for the children for a week past," added Mr O'Neville, "and all the trace we found of them was a dead rabbit which they had been trying to eat. We are very anxious that no harm may come to them in the bush."

"We go kukarda," said Molly as she picked up her fruit

tin and emptied the contents on the patch of grass outside their shelter. "But we'll fill our tins first."

Molly noticed that a few metres along the track was a pool of murky brown water trapped in the clay soil. It looked alright but was it drinkable, she wanted to know. She dipped her hands in and sipped the water. Yes, despite its colour, it was alright.

Leaving the bushlands, they entered the cleared farmlands of the northern wheatbelt. Another farmhouse was in sight. Soon they were approaching the house very cautiously, and using the same routine as before, the girls were supplied with enough food to last them for a few more days.

Contented and with full stomachs, the trio trudged on until darkness fell and they made a shelter for the night. Since their escape, Molly, Daisy and Gracie had cut down their sleeping hours from sunset to first light or piccaninny dawn; a pattern they intended to use all the way home.

That evening, the runaways chattered quietly around the fire before snuggling into their bush shelter to sleep. They talked about the countryside through which they had passed, from the woodlands of the majestic marri and wandoo to the banksia trees of the coastal sand plains. They had seen the chocolate-coloured river, they had slopped through the wet swamp lands and dipped their hands into clear pools filled with black tadpoles.

The girls were very interested in the way the water seemed to change colours with the soil. It was milky white in the clay pans and pink or beige in the more coarse gravelled land. But the memories that were to remain in their minds forever were of the "funny trees" that grew around the settlement and the grass trees with their rough black trunks and the tufts of green, rush-like leaves that sprang out from the top of the plant.

That night, Molly shivered as she lay on the ground pondering on the day's events. She realised that they still had a long, long way to go through an unknown part of the country.

The next day, as they skirted the green wheat fields using the fire break as a path, they were able to pass through the paddocks fairly quickly. In one paddock, flocks of sheep and a herd of cows grazed contentedly.

"Oh look, Dgudu," said Gracie excitedly as she pointed to the white lambs in the flock.

The two younger ones oohed and aahed over these beautiful lambs. The girls were delighted by them and they reacted in the same way as little girls everywhere — they wanted to cuddle and fondle the little lambs. Sadly though, they had a big task ahead of them, with miles to go and lots of ground to cover yet.

Daisy and Gracie looked back once more before they descended into another valley, through the wheatfields and uncleared strips of land then towards the red-coloured breakaways in the distance.

Everything was peaceful, the birds were singing and the sun was shining through the fluffy white clouds once more. The rain had ceased and the girls now had plenty of food, but they were experiencing another problem. The scratches on their legs from the prickly bushes had become infected and sore, causing them great discomfort.

They tried not to think about the pain as they climbed into their cosy shelter that night amongst the mallee gums, acacia shrubs and York gums, and quietly listened to the sounds of the bush. The temperature had dropped considerably and a roaring fire would have been most welcome.

As they drifted off to sleep, they heard the barking of a lone fox, followed by the bleating of lambs. After a pause came the deep baas of the ewes, comforting and protecting their young ones from the terrorising fox.

Rising at dawn the next day, the three girls ate their breakfast on the move. They had gone several kilometres when they came upon a large, dead marri gum burning fiercely. They walked around it quickly and disappeared into the shrubs.

Three days after the article was published in the *West Australian,* Constable H.W. Rowbottom of the Dalwallinu police station reported that, "relative to Escape of three Native girls from Moore River Settlement", he had received a telephone message from Mr D.L. Lyons, farmer of East Damboring who stated that, "he had just noticed in the *West Australian* newspaper that three native girls had escaped during the previous week. These children had called at his farm on Saturday and he had given them food, after which they had travelled across his paddocks going east towards Burakin. He questioned them and asked them where they had come from, but they would not tell him. The eldest one was dressed in what appeared to be a khaki military overcoat, and the others had khaki military jackets on." (14.8.1931) Reg. No. 1065

The Eastern District Police Inspector Crawe was notified immediately. Later that afternoon an urgent telegram was received by Constable Rowbottom, from Mr Neville, the Chief Protector of Aborigines, Perth, authorising him to "incur the expenditure to effect their capture". The constable left immediately by car to East Damboring, calling in at all farms along the road to Burakin.

One farmer, Mr Roche junior of Burakin, noticed a fire at the south end of his boundary and wondered what it was. When he investigated the next day, he found that a dead tree had been set on fire, and the tracks of bare feet were visible.

"It was useless to attempt to do any tracking as it rained all Monday night, and the tracks were obliterated," reported Constable Rowbottom.

No one had seen the runaways at the town of Burakin. It was estimated that they had passed by, travelling due east towards the rabbit-proof fence near Ballidu. No fires were reported in the area. The dead tree fire could have been caused by lightning because Molly, Daisy and Grace had been very careful not to let their fires be seen. That is why they lit them in a hole in the middle of their shelters and covered the ashes over before they left.

Within days of the announcement, responses came in from all around. Telegrams and reports were exchanged back and forth. But the girls continued trekking on, unaware of the search parties that were being assembled by the police. They didn't know that they were just a few days ahead of the searchers and their would-be captors.

Within the week, the scratches on their legs had become festering sores. The three girls had been on the run for over a month. They had left the landscape of red loam, mallee gums, acacia trees and green fields and found themselves in a very different countryside; one of red soil, tall, thick mulgas, gidgies and the beautiful, bright green kurrajong trees that stood out against the grey-green colours of the other vegetation. Underneath the shrubs and trees was a green carpet of everlasting flowers in bud ready to bloom in a couple of weeks' time. The green would then be transformed into a blaze of pink, white and yellow papery flowers.

Molly, Daisy and Gracie were very much at home in this part of the country. They evaded capture by practising survival skills inherited from their nomadic ancestors.

"My legs are sore, Dgudu," cried Gracie. "I can't walk."

"My legs hurt too," chimed in Daisy.

"Mine are sore, too," said Molly. "But we can't hang around here all day, we gotta walk on further."

"I'll carry Daisy first, have a rest then it will be your turn, Gracie," said Molly.

"Alright," both agreed.

The progress was slow and laborious but they persisted. When Molly's turn came to have a break from carrying them, the younger sisters took turns piggy-backing each other.

To fool possible informants, they would approach a farmhouse or a station homestead from one direction and pretend to go off in the opposite way. Then they would do a full circle, making sure that no one was following them, and double back when all was clear and continue along their usual route. But they never ventured too close to any towns throughout the Upper Murchinson district.

One late afternoon, the girls were enjoying the mild winter day, with the sun shining on their backs. It was the kind of day when you felt happy to be alive. The absconders gleaned all the positive energy from the environment, from everything that lived and breathed around them. It would have been perfect if only their legs hadn't been so painful and they had something to eat. Molly was out in front of the other two when she crouched down suddenly amongst some thick prickly kurrara trees and picked up a small stone and threw it at Daisy and Gracie. They had stopped to dig a hole under a large mulga tree. When they looked up, she signalled to them to come to her and sit down.

"Look over there, a station out-camp," whispered Molly. "Go in there and look for some food."

The two youngsters were used to this kind of request. When it came to obtaining food, they never sneaked or crept up to the places — the frontal direct approach was their method. Molly watched them from the safety of the trees and shrubs, as they walked up to the shed. Daisy peeped through a crack in the wooden door and saw the shed was unoccupied.

"Come on," she called to Gracie. "There's nobody in there," she added as she unbolted the door and entered.

Inside the camp, which was merely a tin shed with a bough shelter in front of it, were two camp beds, a table and empty four-gallon tins scattered about in an untidy mess. Daisy and Gracie quickly searched the shelves and the table and found some matches, flour, salt and three large Sunshine milk tins.

Removing the lids with a butcher's knife, which they had found on a rough bench, they were immediately overcome by the appetising aroma of dgingi, the tins were filled with dripping. They couldn't remember when they had smelt this last. They hadn't eaten since breakfast and they were very hungry, so they dipped both hands into the tin and scooped up as much fat as they could and ate it.

"This tastes really good," said Daisy, as she dipped in once again.

"We gotta hurry up," Gracie reminded her sister as she snatched up some of the precious finds.

"Come on," she urged and she rushed out through the door. Daisy spied a billy can underneath the table. She grabbed it and the remaining items and joined the other two outside.

They got as far as the kurrara trees where Molly was waiting for them, when both girls simply doubled over and vomited. When Molly heard what they had done she said, "You silly beggars, you shouldn't eat that dgingi by itself. See you both get sick now." She waited impatiently for the two little girls to finish emptying the dripping from their stomachs.

"Are you alright?" she asked them. They nodded in reply. "Well, come on. Let's move along."

Daisy and Gracie recovered enough to straighten up and take their position behind their older sister who was striding on towards the rabbit-proof fence.

That evening they supped on hot damper, which was made on a clean spare frock, and sweet black tea, then they slept in a dry gully. Their simple meals were just like the ones they ate at home — especially when they managed to find birds, birds' eggs, rabbits and lizards to supplement their meagre diet. But their festering sores were still aching and they could find no relief. Despite the pain they pressed on using the same procedure as before; taking it in turns to carry each other — except Molly who was heavier and bigger than the other two.

One day about midday, when the sun was high in the azure sky, Daisy and Gracie heard an excited shriek from Molly who, as usual, was walking ahead of them.

"Here it is. I've found it. Come and look," she yelled as she laughed and waved her arms.

"What is it?" asked Gracie. "What are you shouting for?"

"I've found the rabbit-proof fence. See," she said, pointing to the fence. "This will take us all the way home to Jigalong."

"But how do you know that's the rabbit-proof fence, Dgudu?" asked Daisy, with a puzzled look on her face. She didn't notice anything special about this fence.

"This fence is straight, see," Molly explained. "And it's clear on each side of the fence."

She should know, after all her father was the inspector of the fence and he told her all about it. Now the fence would help her and her sisters find their way home. There was much excitement when the girls at last reached the rabbit-proof fence.

From when she was young, Molly had learned that the fence was an important landmark for the Mardudjara people of the Western Desert who migrated south from the remote regions. They knew that once they reached Billanooka Station, it was simply a matter of following the rabbit-proof fence to their final destination, the Jigalong government depot; the desert outpost of the white man. The fence cut through the country from south to north. It was a typical response by the white people to a problem of their own making. Building a fence to keep the rabbits out proved to be a futile attempt by the government of the day.

For the three runaways, the fence was a symbol of love, home and security.

"We're nearly home," said Molly without realising that

they had merely reached the halfway mark, they had almost eight hundred kilometres still to go.

"We found the fence now. It gunna be easy," she told her younger sisters. They were glad to hear that because each morning when they awoke they were never sure whether they would survive another day.

Molly was determined to reach Jigalong and nothing was going to stop her. She renewed her vow as she greeted the fence like a long-lost friend, touching and gripping the cold wire.

"We gunna walk alongside it all the way to Jigalong," Molly said confidently. It would stand out like a beacon that would lead them out of the rugged wilderness, across a strange country to their homeland.

"They must have had plenty of rain around this country," said Molly as they tramped through the tall green grass. It was difficult to imagine that within a few weeks this landscape would be transformed into a mass of colour and beauty as pink, white and yellow everlasting flowers bloomed. These would cover the red earth and delight any travellers who passed through. But the three girls would not have that pleasure as they would be miles away by then, out of the Murchinson and into the Pilbara region.

By mid-afternoon, they entered a clearing amongst the mulga and gidgi trees and found some murrandu holes that appeared promising. But at that very moment, they heard a man yelling out to them. "Hey, you girls. Wait." The voice came from down the track along the fence.

They saw an Aboriginal man riding a bike. The three dashed into the bush forgetting the pain of the sores on their legs.

"Don't run away. I want to talk to you," he shouted. Peeping out from the thick acacia bushes they saw that he was holding something in one hand as he pedalled with great difficulty. "Look, I've got some food to give you. See," he said. "Come on, don't be frightened."

Their need and desire for food overcame fear and caution. The man's name was Don and he explained that he worked on Pindathuna Station. He shared his lunch of tinned meat and bread with them and gave them a box of matches.

"Where are you going?" he asked them.

"We gunna follow the railway line to Wiluna," said Molly.

Stockman Don Willocks reported the incident to his boss. Mr A.H. Gillam telephoned Constable Robert Larsen at the Yalgoo police station who reported that:

> one of his stockmen, Don Willocks, had reported to him that he had seen tracks in one of the Pindathuna paddocks which appeared to have been made by two females. He followed the tracks on 4/9/31 and came up with three female half-castes who were travelling north along the rabbit-proof fence. He then ascertained that ... one was about 8 years of age and the other two older. They were all dressed in khaki dresses and dark overcoats and were carrying a bundle and a billycan. Original Police No. 5979/31 Reg. No. 1163

Don Willocks had noticed signs of the girls three days earlier in one of the Pindathuna paddocks, but he saw only two sets of tracks which indicated that, "they were in a bad way, as in places they appeared to be dragging their feet and that he thought inquiries should be made".

However, when he caught up with them, he was pleased to notice, "that there was nothing wrong with them". He found that there were three of them and that two were carrying one girl between them.

Constable Robert Larsen of the Yalgoo police station, had led an earlier search party for the girls and so he was keen to follow up these reported sightings. At last he would be able to inform Inspector Simpson at the Geraldton police station that some contact had been made with the girls.

A tracker named Ben from Noongal Station was brought

into the search and he and Larsen travelled to Pindathuna to pick up Willocks on 5 September 1931. It was impossible for the men to find the tracks because heavy rains the night before had washed them away. Nevertheless, the search party proceeded along the rabbit-proof fence for a few kilometres, searching for tracks as they went. Finding none they continued parallel with the fence until dark then made a camp. At dawn the next morning they continued their search and came upon fresh tracks. Finally, however, Larsen recorded that the tracking was discontinued "owing to the tracker having sore feet, myself having to attend the Police Court on Monday 7/9/31. I decided to return to Yalgoo".

Constable Larsen, Don Willocks and Ben, the Aboriginal tracker, left the tracks about 28 kilometres north of Dalgaranga Station. What they didn't know was that the three runaways had climbed over the rabbit-proof fence and doubled back to pick up some bush tucker and return the same way.

In his report to Inspector Simpson, Larsen wrote:

> Apparently these girls are following the fence going to Nullagine, and could probably be picked up at the next junction. No doubt seeing Willocks on the Pindathuna run frightened the girls, thinking that he would probably report the matter. I am of the opinion that they will settle down when they get further up the fence, as it would be impossible for them to keep travelling at the same pace on the 5th and 6th inst. having travelled about 40 miles in two days. (Original Police No. 5979/31 Reg. No. 1163.)

Molly, Daisy and Gracie realised that although they were in familiar territory they were not safe from the authorities. The girls knew that they could be captured at any time of the day or night and be sent all the way back to the settlement. It was too risky even to stop to light a fire to cook their murrandu.

By early September, the police were increasing their

efforts to find the girls and any information they collected was passed on to other officers stationed further north. Constable Summers, for example, notified Constable Fanning by railway phone on 8 September that the girls were following the fence and would probably be going near Nannine and Gumtree Creek.

Constable Larsen kept Inspector Louis Simpson informed about the search. "The Tracker Ben is of the opinion that if these girls come in contact with the Sandstone blacks they will be done away with as they will not stand any other natives in their country, as they are a very treacherous tribe."

The girls had been on the run for five weeks and were surviving on bush tucker and water. They would sleep for only a few hours under bushes as they were aware that they could be caught following their contact with Don Willocks. They purposely avoided station homesteads and despite the cold nights no fire was lit.

> Unless these girls are intercepted I am afraid that they are in for a very bad time after they pass Gum Creek on the old Nannine–Wiluna Road. I feel sure that the girls will stick to the No.8 rabbit-proof fence until it junctions with No.1 rabbit-proof fence going towards Nullagine. Water and native game should be abundant at this time of the year, but as the girls get further to the north I fear for their safety.

Thus reported Louis D. Simpson, Inspector of Police, Geraldton on 10 September 1931.

One day in a clearing close to the fence, the girls spied an emu and a family of six tiny black and white striped chicks strolling along behind him. While Daisy stood perfectly still behind some trees, Molly and Gracie chased and captured a chick each. The old man emu turned on them but gave up when he remembered that the other four chicks were unprotected.

The three girls waited in the seclusion of the small acacia

bushes to see if anyone would come to investigate the commotion, but no one appeared so they plucked and cooked the emu chicks for supper, accompanied by damper and washed down with black bitter tea; there was no sugar left.

After supper they slept under some thick shrubs. That night Molly dreamed that she and her younger sisters were being pursued by a policeman and a black tracker on a horse. She could see them riding beside the fence on magnificent grey stallions, coming towards them from the north. They were coming closer, and closer — at that critical moment she woke up shaking with fear and covered in sweat. Then she heard them. It wasn't a dream after all. It was real. Clop, clop, clopping of the horses came.

Molly shook the other two awake. "Keep still and don't make a noise," she whispered, shivering slightly. "It might be a policeman and that Mardu tracker."

They lay on their stomachs, not daring to move and watched sleepily as the riders passed slowly by them.

Molly sat up and sighed with relief and said, "They're only station yowadas, not policemen."

It was still dark with the first rays of dawn only just appearing in the eastern sky. The birds began twittering and fluttering through the trees and bushes around them.

"We'll eat on the run," said Molly, and they headed towards Meekatharra.

Soon they were on the outskirts of the town where they could hear the sounds of people going about their business, the shunting of the goods train, and other noises unfamiliar to these girls from the desert area.

"Dgudu, let us go into Meekatharra and ask somebody to give us midka for the road," Gracie suggested. "That old lady Minnie, you know the one who used to be on Ethel Creek Station, the one married to that old man from Nullagine. She will help us," she added hopefully.

"No," snapped Molly. "There're policemen in that town.

They will pick us up and send us to Moore River," she reminded Gracie. "No, we go around Meekatharra."

Daisy said nothing, she was used to them bickering and squabbling, so she didn't let any of it bother her at all.

A week later on 13 September, Constable T.R. Penn of the Meekatharra police station, accompanied by a tracker named Jacky, left the station, "in a private motor car and proceeded along the Meekatharra–Nannine Road to where the No. 5 rabbit-proof fence intersects it. We made a thorough search in this vicinity, along the road and up and down the fence for tracks and through the surrounding bush but found no trace." Original Police No. 5979/31 Reg. No. 1520

The men searched on either side of the fence and a considerable distance from it in the Annean Station for about 16 kilometres in very rough country until nightfall when they set up camp.

The next morning the pair continued the search. Travelling in this rough country is always difficult and hazardous, however, but with the heavy rains it was impossible to proceed any further by car. Constable Penn returned to Meekatharra at 9.30 am on the 15 September after making a "thorough search along the road for about two miles north and south of the fence in case the girls crossed the road further away from the fence and surrounding bush".

The girls' spirits soared as they realised that home was drawing nearer and nearer each day. They had reached the railway siding near Mt Russel Station quite unexpectedly several days after passing near the town of Meekatharra. It was here that Gracie decided that she had had enough of trekking in the wilderness and living off bush tucker. She'd had her fill of this arduous venture.

"I'm going to the station to see those people working over there," a determined Gracie told her sisters. Fifteen minutes later she returned to announce her decision. "That woman, the muda-muda one working here told me that my mummy left Walgun Station and is living in Wiluna," she said excitedly. "I am going with her when the train comes."

Gracie was just plain tired and weary of walking; her bare feet were very sore. Looking at the endless posts and wire that made up the rabbit-proof fence became too much for her. She flatly refused to go any further.

"I don't want to die," she said finally as she turned her back to walk away from them. "I'm going to my mummy in Wiluna."

The pleadings and beggings of her sisters fell on deaf ears. For Gracie it was easier to hop on a train than to trudge on further to Jigalong.

Molly and Daisy lingered for as long as they dared before they accepted Gracie's parting. Then they continued north on their incredible journey to reach their goal, that lonely isolated outpost on the edge of the desert.

Molly found Gracie's decision very hard to accept, but she agreed with her younger sister in the end that it was closer to Wiluna than it was to Jigalong.

By noon on the day they parted, the temperature had risen and it was the hottest day since their abscondment. The military coat and jackets were discarded and Molly and Daisy decided to rest beside a creekbed. There wasn't much water in it but there was enough to quench their thirst and to fill their billy can, so that they would have a supply of drinking water until they came across a windmill or one of the wells along the Canning Stock Route.

Molly was exhausted, not only from the trekking and the lack of sleep, but the argument with Gracie had left her emotionally drained. So she found a soft spot near the creek, clear of rocks and stones, and making herself comfortable she dozed off to sleep.

Daisy had discovered a bird's nest in a river gum on the bank. It was a pink and white cockatoo's nest with four young squawking chicks in it. While her older sister slept

Daisy climped up and grabbed three of the chicks, one by one, and killed them by wringing their scrawny necks, then dropped them onto the ground. As she was reaching for the last chick, she slipped and grazed her knee. It was very painful so she rubbed it to soothe the stinging. There was no relief so she became quite angry and swore loudly to herself, which didn't stop the pain but it made her feel better.

Suddenly she was disturbed by a man's voice.

"Hey, where's your big sister?"

"What?" answered Daisy as she turned around to the speaker, a young man, a muda-muda dressed in station workers clothes, standing on the rocky outcrop near a larger river gum.

"I said, Where's your big sister?" he yelled. "Tell her to come here to me. I want her. I heard about you girls, you ran away from the settlement. Yeah, Moore River," he added as he swaggered towards her.

Daisy was still smarting from the knee injury and let out a string of abuse, swearing in both English and Mardu wangka, telling him exactly what to do with himself. Then she bent down and picked up some big stones and pelted him with them.

He ran, ducking and weaving, to avoid the missiles that were being hurled at him. As the young stockman mounted his horse he yelled back angrily, "Awright, you bitch, you wait. I gunna report you to the police."

Molly came running, awakened by the shouting and swearing. "What's wrong?" she asked. "Who are you swearing at?" When Daisy had finished explaining what had occurred, Molly cursed.

"The mongrel bastard," she said, feeling very threatened. A man who had been spurned and attacked by a small girl might just carry out his threat.

"Come on, we'd better move along," urged Molly.

So they picked up the chicks and plucked them as they

walked over the stony surface of the rugged red plains. The girls didn't stop until nightfall, when the shadows were long and they felt it was safe to make a fire to cook the birds.

Since the confrontation with the station hand, the two sisters became even more cautious. They were taking no chances at this stage of the trek as they were so close to home.

With the change of climate the girls were able to take advantage of the longer hours of daylight. They were able to rise early and cover a good distance before nightfall. They were now in their own land and they knew exactly where they were heading.

Just south of Station 594, along the Canning Stock Route, they discovered a burrow with fresh tracks leading to it. They realised that it wasn't made by rabbits, but by a cat, a feral cat. Molly grabbed a thick stick and began digging while Daisy stood by to clobber it with her stick.

The fat cat spat and scratched Molly's arms and neck but that didn't deter her. That evening they had feral cat for supper, and some for breakfast the next morning.

Molly and Daisy were relieved when they climbed through the southern boundary fence of Station 594, or as it was known by the local people — '94. It was a cattle station along the Canning Stock Route, south of Jigalong. By this time all the flour, tea and water had been used so they forced themselves to walk faster and make an effort to reach the windmill south of the station.

That night they had no supper but they filled up with water until they were bloated and very uncomfortable. As they couldn't sleep, the girls decided to continue walking towards the station while the moon was full and shining brightly. Eventually, weariness forced them to stop and they made themselves as comfortable as they could on the rough sand of a creekbed and fell asleep immediately.

Molly and Daisy woke at piccaninny dawn and were driven by pangs of hunger to Station 594. When they saw the camp site they almost ran but they didn't have the energy. They knew exactly where to find their aunt's camp as they had both been there before. Their aunt, Molly's step-father's sister, greeted them in the traditional manner by crying with them and for those who had passed away since their last meeting.

"Where did you girls come from? Where have you been?" she asked. Their aunt and other relations couldn't believe what the girls told them. They were amazed and intrigued by their story.

"You poor silly girls, you could have died in the bush somewhere and no one would have known." She began to cry loudly.

The two sisters sank gratefully into the warm bath their aunt prepared for them; their first since leaving the East Perth Girls Home. They had grown used to washing themselves at the windmills and pools along the way. The supper of beef stew, home-made bread and tea revived them. Their aunt heaped their plates with stew but Molly and Daisy found that they could only manage small quantities of food as their stomachs had shrunk during their trek.

"Don't worry about that," said their aunt warmly. "You'll soon be fixed when you get back to your mummies. They will fatten you up again. You're too skinny."

After supper they all sat around the fire, sharing some of their experiences with their relations late into the night. Then both stretched out on comfortable beds and fell sound asleep.

The two sisters awoke the next day feeling refreshed and rested after the good night's sleep. In fact, they felt that they could complete the last leg of their journey without the constant fear of capture or starvation.

"Not far to go, Dgudu," said Daisy.

"No, not far now. We'll be home soon," replied Molly.

They would have reached their goal within the next three or four days. These two girls had overcome their fears and proved that they could survive. It took a strong will and a purpose — they had both.

For the first time in seven weeks the sisters didn't have to rush or eat on the run. They found it very pleasant to have breakfast later instead of rising at first light, and they took their time to enjoy the small pieces of juicy pan-fried steaks, hot damper and tea sweetened with Nestles milk that their aunt had prepared for them.

When they had almost finished breakfast, their cousin Joey came over and joined them and accepted a mug of tea.

"We're going back to Jigalong this morning as soon as the boss finishes his breakfast," he said.

Molly and Daisy were ready in a few minutes and sat waiting for Joey's signal. They didn't have to wait long. Picking up their calico bags, which were now the same colour as the red earth, they walked purposely towards Joey and his boss. They turned and waved goodbye to their aunt and cousin, the others were still asleep, and joined the maintenance workers of the rabbit-proof fence.

"You two girls can take it in turns riding this camel back to Jigalong," said Ron Clarkson, the contract worker, as he patted the animal. The camel raised its head, looking around everywhere and chewing without pausing. Ron returned to the other camel that he normally rode.

Daisy nudged her older sister and pointing to the camel, whispered, "Is this a man or woman one, Dgudu?"

"I don't know yet. I can't tell while it's lying down. Wait till it stands up, then I'll tell you."

The girls had seen the cheeky, spitting, biting camels at the depot and didn't like them one bit.

"You go first, I'll walk and we'll change over when I get tired, alright," said Molly as she helped Daisy onto the camel's back.

"Yeah, alright then," said Daisy, giving the animal the correct commands as instructed by Ron Clarkson.

"It's a woman camel," Molly informed her. Both were

relieved that they weren't given a nasty, bad tempered, spitting bull camel.

"Ready to move along?" asked the boss.

"Yes," they replied, and followed him slowly out through the station gates and across the stone covered plains, scattered with spinifex grass, acacia bushes and spindly mulga trees, towards the rabbit-proof fence.

Daisy enjoyed the ride and welcomed the chance at last to watch the passing scenery from above ground level.

The first break was beside Lake Nabberu between Station 494 and Mundwindi Station. After a lunch of grilled steak, damper and tea, the four travellers rested in the cool shade of the river gums until mid-afternoon.

At sunset, they entered the camp of Bob George, the owner of 494 Station, and his wife Ibby, that was set up near the rabbit-proof fence. Here they ate and camped the night. At seven o'clock the next morning they continued their journey northwards.

The sun was setting the following evening when they entered the main gate to Munda Mindi, several kilometres to the left of the rabbit-proof fence and made a camp.

"You three stay here. I'll be back soon," Ron Clarkson told them, as he tied his camel to the fence.

Joey, Molly and Daisy set about gathering wood for a fire and sat down and listened while Joey brought them up to date with the latest news and family gossip. Half an hour later, Joey's boss returned carrying a cardboard box of homemade bread, boiled cold potatoes, tins of corn beef and a canvas bag of water.

"Here, you can make your own tea, alright." The three nodded. Joey untied his billy can from his swag and filled it with water from the water bag and put it on the fire. Molly and Daisy agreed that this was the best supper yet.

After their meal, they sat around the blazing fire and yarned until they grew weary and settled down to a peaceful sleep near the fire, sharing a blanket between them. Soon they would be reunited with their mothers, just as their sister Gracie had been. That night they slept a dreamless sleep.

For breakfast the following morning they ate bread and jam, salted beef and sweet, black tea, which they thoroughly enjoyed. Molly took her turn to ride while Daisy walked beside her.

They were passing through country that was familiar to Daisy, so she took great delight and pleasure showing her big sister all the places where her family had camped and where bush tucker was plentiful. Her step-father and uncles always managed to bring home more than enough for the whole family.

Molly, Daisy, Joey and Ron Clarkson lunched and rested on the banks of Savory Creek, quite near where Molly was born, then facing north they made tracks for home. It felt wonderful.

One late afternoon in October 1931, the four travelled silently across the plains along the rabbit-proof fence, each one deep in their own thoughts. The silence was broken occasionally by the cawing of crows and the swishing of the camels' tails as they brushed away the scores of pesky bush flies. These insects attached themselves to the dusty travellers and hitched a ride all the way to the end of their journey.

The late afternoon was pleasantly warm, though the nights were still rather cool.

Now it was Molly's turn to point out special places to Daisy. It was a quick trip down memory's landscape. They passed close to the claypan where Molly was born. A feeling of nostalgia brought tears to her eyes as memories of her childhood flashed before her.

"You can get up now," said Molly. She was tired of sitting on the camel's back.

"Alright," said Daisy eagerly, she didn't mind riding the rest of the way.

As they drew closer, nervous excitement was building up inside them. Both girls took in the familiar landscape of the red earth, the dry spinifex grass and grey-green mulga trees. There was nothing to compare with the beauty of these plains that stretched out in all directions.

They could see the black hills in the distance where their families hunted for girdi-girdis and murrandus. They were approaching the camp site now, the dogs were barking and people were shouting to each other and pointing in their direction. Some were sitting in the creekbed, wailing quietly. But all eyes were focussed on the four weary travellers. Unbeknown to them, their Uncle Freddie had ridden on ahead to tell the old people that Molly and Daisy were returning home to them.

The four travellers parted company on the banks of the Jigalong Creek, close to the mud-brick huts of the depot, and made their way to their homes. The girls walked slowly towards their mothers' camps where their family sat awaiting their arrival.

The wailing began softly at first then grew louder as more people joined the group.

The maintenance boss called out just before he disappeared behind the huts. "Come down to the store and get some rations, alright."

"Yeah, alright," they replied shyly. But neither of the girls accepted that offer because at daybreak the next morning, their families moved away from the depot and had no intention of returning until they were absolutely certain that the girls were safe from government officers and policemen.

Molly and Daisy did not relish the idea of being sent back to the Moore River Native Settlement. The trek had been no easy feat. It had taken the girls months to complete and nothing or nobody could take this moment of happiness and satisfaction from them. They had finally reached their destination and were reunited with their families. They had taken a great risk. Inmates absconding from the settlement were considered to be a serious problem. If they had been caught, the girls would have had their heads shaved or made to wear sacks and other more serious punishments.

The task of apprehending Molly and Daisy was handed back to Constable M.J. Riggs of the Nullagine police station. This was the policeman, who in his role as a Protection Officer, had removed the three girls from Jigalong and escorted them to Marble Bar. Now he was informing the Commission of Police that, "From inquiries made I am of the opinion that the girls will not return to Jigalong for a while, but that they will stay around Lake Naboroo with the natives in the vicinity ..." (4/12/1931. Police File No. 5979/31.)

The correspondence concerning the girls continued.

I heard from the Constable in charge at Nullagine that the three half-caste girls have not yet been recovered.

I am afraid you will never get them now as by this time they will be back in their own country and well and truly camouflaged; even if you did fluke them now, I do not think you would ever keep them unless you separated them all or locked them up, but of course that latter course would be worse than their being in the bush I guess.

Yours faithfully
Arthur T. Hungerford
Protector of Aborigines
Jigalong Depot 11/10/31

Mr A.O. Neville
The Chief Protector of Aborigines

Dear Sir,
    Re:173/30

The half-castes Molly and Daisy are back in this locality now and seem none the worse for their most wonderful "trek". I expect they did walk in record time considering they had to most of the time provide their own food ..."

Arthur T. Hungerford
Jigalong 29/12/31

Quite recently the two girls were in the native camp at 494 Gate on the rabbit-proof fence, and about 123 miles from here. Molly — I was informed by Mrs R. George (half-caste) — has gone back to Jigalong. Daisy has gone with an uncle named Peter. This native, I understand, is a bush native and it is very unlikely they will go to Lake Nabery as this is about sixty miles south of Georges' camp at 494.

(Signed) E. Morrow
Constable 1302

To the Chief Protector of Aborigines, Nullagine.

Molly, one of the half-caste girls who decamped from Moore River Native Settlement has been seen in this locality. Do you want her sent back down south?

Constable Riggs

The Chief Protector of Aborigines has informed the Commissioner of Police that he did not desire any further action in re: half-caste Molly because she has been a costly woman to the Department. Very heavy expenditure was incurred in securing her, and when she decamped a lot of undesirable publicity took place.

The Commissioner of Aboriginal Affairs
(File No. 345/36)

Mr A.O. Neville
Chief Protector of Aborigines

Dear Sir,
Constable Riggs told me you were not bothering about the half-caste Molly, does the same apply to Daisy? I hear they are

back somewhere in their own country though goodness knows where.

Yours faithfully
Arthur T. Hungerford
Jigalong 5/11/31

I would like the child to be recovered if no great expense is to be incurred; otherwise the prestige of the Department is likely to suffer.

Mr A.O. Neville
(21/10/31. File 175/30)

Gracie, or Chrissy as she was called by the authorities, remained at the railway siding intending to catch the weekly train to Wiluna. When she was told that she had to wait for a couple of days however, she took off early the next morning following the railway until she came to a place called White Well where a Mardu couple named Rosie and Ned were camped.

"Come and have something to eat and rest," invited Rosie. "What's your name and where do you come from?"

"I am Lucy from Jigalong," said Gracie. When the train arrived Ned, Rosie and Gracie travelled to Wiluna.

In no time at all, Gracie was enjoying the relaxed, casual lifestyle she led before her transportation south. Although she had trouble settling down in one place and sleeping in the same bed every night on a mattress.

Her mother was not at Wiluna when she arrived but Gracie was prepared to wait until she came to fetch her. In the meantime she was growing accustomed to having all the comforts of home, three full meals a day and a comfortable bed to sleep on.

One day when she was sitting outside at the camp she was spotted by an informer, a Mardu police tracker. He rushed back to the police station and reported to Sergeant James Mills.

"Sergeant, you know those three muda-muda girls that ran away from the settlement?"

"Yes. I remember the telegrams and information about them."

"Well, I saw one of them at Rosie and Ned's camp."

"What?" he exclaimed. "You mean to tell me that they actually walked to here."

"No, only one," said the tracker.

Sergeant Mills drove over to the camp to interview Gracie who "stated that her name was Lucy, and that she and two other girls ran away from the Jigalong Station, and they all walked to White Well 40 miles from Wiluna and the other girls then went bush and left her behind and when the train came along on the 26/9/31 she came to Wiluna". (File 173/30.)

"This girl Lucy, he informed the Chief Protector of Aborigines, "is approximately about 12 or 13 years of age and about half grown ... and is very shy and timid. She doesn't belong to this district, and was inclined to run away into the bush from Rosie's camp, so I brought her to the Police Station on the 4/10/31 and I am keeping her here until I receive instructions from you." (James Mills, Sgt. 3/C807, Wiluna 5/10/31)

"Can you identify girl called Lucy. Either Daisy thirteen formerly with Mrs Chellow, Murra Munda or Molly fourteen, Chrissy eleven from Jigalong," telegrammed the Chief Protector of Aborigines on 13 October.

"Chrissy is the name of girl I have here please advise," Sergeant Mills replied.

All the officials concerned agreed that Gracie should be returned to the settlement as soon as possible. Neville, the Chief Protector of Aborigines, tried to avoid expenditure, however, so he welcomed the suggestions made by Sergeant Mills and Inspector Simpson. Sergeant Mills proposed that his wife escort Gracie on the condition that the Chief Protector's Department pay the fare and expenses. "We'll pay the fare but not the expenses," replied the Chief Protector.

Finally, Neville notified the Commissioner of Police, "that approval is hereby given to bring the half-caste girl 'Chrissy' down. She is to be accompanied by Mrs Mills as suggested in his report on the 21/10/31. Please advise when the child can be expected to reach Mogumber." (File No. 173/30.)

When the Chief Protector received the invoice from Sergeant Mills he pleaded with him that, "in such a case as this you might make a reduction in the amount charged for meals on account of the half-caste girl 'Chrissy'? The Department is in an unfortunate position in this respect as it cannot make other arrangements which might result in board being provided at a cheaper rate. Admittedly the case is exceptional but it is quite feasible that the child might have been provided for at a lesser rate elsewhere." (File 173/30, 23/1/32)

Sergeant Mills replied curtly that

> I cannot possibly see my way clear to make any reduction in the attached account. The cost of living is very high here, and I make no profit at all of meals supplied at one shilling each, and besides my wife has to cook and prepare them and she is entitled to something for this labour.
>
> When I took charge of this girl she was nearly starving and therefore a big eater for the first few weeks. She had very few clothes and my wife found the material and made clothes for her, which went with her when she left here.
>
> It was no fault of mine that she was there for over ten weeks and I advised you on several occasions that it was inconvenient for me to have her here. So under the circumstances I think this account is very reasonable seeing that she got board, lodgings and clothes for twenty shillings per week.
>
> I would be much obliged if you can see your way clear to

expedite the payment of this account. (Jas. Mills, Sgt 3/C807, 27/1/32, Wiluna File 173/30)

The total sum paid to the policemen involved in the search and recapturing of the three runaways from Jigalong was quite handsome. The three of them put the Department "in an unfortunate position" financially. In a letter to the Commissioner of Police, the Chief Protector of Aborigines stated that:

It's a pity that those youngsters have gone "native" [he's referring to Molly and Daisy], but it cannot be helped. They were attractive children, and ought to have been brought in years ago.

This emphasises the necessity for Police Officers to report the presence of half-caste children in the bush. I know this is done now, but it seems to have been neglected in some districts in the past.

Chief Protector of Aborigines
26/4/32
(File No. 175/30)

"We followed that fence, the rabbit-proof fence, all the way home from the settlement to Jigalong. Long way, alright. We stay in the bush hiding there for a long time," remembers Molly, who is in her late seventies. When she was only fourteen years old she decided that she wanted to have a part in planning her own destiny.

"Long way" sums up rather understatedly what was, without a doubt, one of the longest walks in the history of the Australian outback. While other parts of this vast country of ours have been crossed on horses or camels, these three girls did their exploring on their bare feet. An incredible achievement in anyone's language. The vastness and the diversity of the Western Australian landscape would always be respected and appreciated by them — they trekked across it and conquered. This historic trek had taken almost nine weeks.

Several months later a small group of people were relaxing around a fire in the lounge room of a boarding house in the south-west town of Margaret River. They were listening with great interest while some young women were relating a tragic incident where three Aboriginal girls were either drowned in the raging floods or perished in the wilderness, but their bodies were never found.

"Where did this happen?" asked a lady named Mrs Mary Dunnet, who was holidaying with her sister — the proprietor of the boarding house.

"At the Moore River Native Settlement near Mogumber north of Perth," was the reply. The women recounting the story were employed as nurses there at the time the incident occurred.

"Well, I am pleased to tell you that those girls didn't drown, they returned home safe and sound to Jigalong and Wiluna," said Mrs Dunnet. Incidently, she later took Molly in as a trainee house maid on her cattle station, the Balfour Downs Station, about 40 kilometres north-east of the present site of the Jigalong community.

9

What Happened to Them?
Where are They Now?

*Molly Kelly (*nee *Craig)*

Molly was trained and employed as a domestic help on Balfour Downs Station where she married Toby Kelly, a stockman. She had two daughters Doris (the author) and Annabelle. On 18 November 1940, after Molly's discharge from the Royal Perth Hospital where she had undergone surgery for appendicitis, she was transported once again under ministerial warrant to Moore River Native Settlement. Nine months later, Molly received a letter from home advising her of the deaths of members of her family at Jigalong. A niece had died from self-inflicted wounds to the head, a customary action of the distressed and the anguished and a common expression of grief and despair. In this case the lacerations were inflicted when Molly and her children had departed months earlier. Others died from whooping cough.

Permission to return to Balfour Downs was refused. Unable to settle down, Molly absconded on 1 January 1941, taking eighteen-month-old Annabelle (Anna) with her and leaving Doris behind at the settlement. She and her baby daughter arrived safely at Jigalong months later, following the same route she had taken nine years earlier. She moved back to Balfour Downs Station with her husband Toby and baby Annabelle. Three years later Annabelle was removed and sent south to the Sister Kate's Children's Home in Queens Park. Molly has not seen her since. Molly and Toby worked on various stations in the Meekatharra and Newman districts until their retirement in 1972. Toby passed away in October 1973. Molly now lives quietly at Jigalong, although she is still actively involved in community affairs. Under traditional Aboriginal kinship Molly has eighteen grandchildren, 29 great-grandchildren and two great-great grandchildren.

Gracie Cross (nee Fields)

Gracie was captured at Wiluna and was transported back to Moore River Settlement where she was given the surname of Jigalong, later shortened to Long. She completed her education and was sent out to work as domestic help on various farms in the wheatbelt, in institutions in the metropolitan area and on stations in the Murchinson region. While working on a station in the Shark Bay district she married a young station hand named Harry Cross. They had six children: Lucina, Therese, Margaret, Marcia, Celine and Clarence. After their separation, Gracie moved to Geraldton. She passed away in July 1983. Gracie never returned to Jigalong.

Daisy Kadibil

After being reunited with her family, Daisy moved with them to the Jimalbar goldfields then to a camp near Lake Naberu, along the rabbit-proof fence south of Jigalong. She trained as a house maid and was later employed on various stations in the district. She married Kadibil, a station hand,

and had four children: Noreena, Elizabeth, Jenny and Margaret. After her husband's death, Daisy moved to Kalundi Seventh Day Adventist Mission, 25 kilometres north of Meekatharra, where she worked as a cook–house-keeper. She remained there until the mission closed in the 1970s. Daisy is a wonderful storyteller. This book may not have been written had it not been for her skill and love for storytelling, her vivid memory and her zest for life. Daisy now lives with her son and daughters and their families at Jigalong.

Glossary of Mardujara words*

barlu, him, her, that person
biguda, red kangaroo
buchiman, bushman
bukala, hurry
bilgurs, betrothed or promised man
bunna, ground or earth, sand
dgingi, fat or dripping
dgudu, older sister
dgundu, dingo or dog
durn-durns, young girl or adolescent
galyu time, rainy season
gengas, spirit of the ancestors
gilla, rainbow snake
girdi girdi, hill kangaroo
gulja, a mixture of tobacco and ashes
gulu, wait
gurnmanu, what's his name
indi, isn't it
jaarta, shirt
jawuja, trousers
jina, foot
jina jina, dress, frock or shirt
kudda, hair

*also spelt Mardudjara, Martujara

kukarda, east
kyalie, north
make kumbu, urinate
marbarn, object of magical powers for healing or finding lost items
marbu, flesh-eating spirit (also **marlbu**)
mayi, damper
midgerji, white woman
midgi-midgi, red
midka, food, a meal or feast
muda-muda, half-caste
mundu, meat
murrandu, goanna (also **murrundu**)
neked, naked
ngubby, thing, something
pink-eye time, summer, holiday time
wandi, a female
wangka, to talk, language
worru, fire
wudgebulla, white man
wuungku, a shelter (also **wuundu**)
yaata, go away
yalta or galyu time, winter or the rainy season
yardini, come here
yina booger, footwear
youay, yes
yowada, horse

References

Books

Biskup, P., 1973, *Not Slaves: Not Citizens,* University of Queensland Press, St Lucia.

Crowley, F.K. and de Garis, B.K., *A Short History of Western Australia,* Melbourne and Sydney.

Hughes, R., 1988, *The Fatal Shore,* Pan Books, London.

Moore, G.F., *Diary of Ten Years of an Early Settler in Western Australia,* University of Western Australia Press, Perth.

Rowley, C.D., 1970, *The Destruction of Aboriginal Society,* Australian National University Press, Canberra.

——, 1971, *Outcasts in White Australia,* Australian National University Press, Canberra.

——, 1971, *The Remote Aborigines,* Australian National University Press, Canberra.

Stone, S.N., 1974, *Aborigines in White Australia,* Griffen Press, Adelaide.

Tonkinson, R., 1974, *The Jigalong Mob: Aboriginal Victors of The Desert Crusade,* Benjamin/Collins, California.

——, 1978, *The Mardudjara Aborigines: Living the Dream in Australia's Desert,* Holt, Rinehart and Winston, Sydney.

Government Records and Newspapers

Department of Family and Children's Services Original Police File Number 5979/31

Department of Native Affairs File Numbers 173/30; 175/30; 345/36

Illustrated Melbourne Post 20 August, 1861

⁎ Australian 11 August, 1931